BTEC Introduction

Sport & Leisure

Ray Barker
Bob Harris
Louise Sutton

www.heinemann.co.uk
✓ Free online support
✓ Useful weblinks
✓ 24 hour online ordering

01865 888058

Heinemann
Inspiring generations

Heinemann is an imprint of Pearson Education Limited, a company incorporated in England and Wales, having its registered office at Edinburgh Gate, Harlow, Essex, CM20 2JE. Registered Company number: 872828

www.heinemann.co.uk

Heinemann is a registered trademark of Pearson Education Limited

Text © Ray Barker, Bob Harris and Louise Sutton, 2005

First published 2005

10 09 08 07 06 05
10 9 8 7 6 5 4 3 2

British Library Cataloguing in Publication Data is available from the British Library on request.

13-digit ISBN 978 0 435460 00 6

Typeset by Saxon Graphics Ltd, Derby

Printed by Scotprint Ltd

Cover photo © Getty Images
Picture research by Ruth Blair / Kath Kollberg
Designed by Lorraine Inglis

Websites

Please note that the examples of websites suggested in this book were up to date at the time of writing. We have made all links available on the Heinemann website at www.heinemann.co.uk/hotlinks. When you access the site, the express code is 0005P.

Contents

Acknowledgements

The authors and publisher are grateful to those who have given permission to reproduce material.

The Royal Borough of Windsor and Maidenhead, p33; Diane Bailey Associates Training Design Consultancy, p40; Advisory, Conciliation and Arbitration Service, p48; NEXT Directory, p144; The Football Association, p200; Birmingham City Council, p237.

Crown copyright material is reproduced under Class Licence No. C02W0005419 with the permission of the Controller of HMSO and the Queen's Printer for Scotland.

Every effort has been made to contact copyright holders of material in this book. Any omissions or errors will be rectified in subsequent printings if notice is given to the publisher.

Photos

Corbis/Arko Datta/Reuters, p2; Corbis/Darren Staples/Reuters, p18; Corbis/Ariel Skelley, p45; Corbis, p72; Corbis/Jim Craigmyle, p83; Getty Images, p100; Sally and Richard Greenhill, p106; Sally and Richard Greenhill, p116; Getty images/Photodisc, p134; Corbis/Reuters, p139; Alamy, p152; Corbis/Reuters, p160; Corbis/Tim Pannell, p175; Getty images/Photodisc, p177; Corbis/Richard Klune, p178; Corbis/LWA-Dann Tardif, p199; Corbis, p202; Corbis/Lawrence Manning, p209; Corbis/Reuters, p210; Getty Images, p227.

Introduction

This book has been written for students who are working towards the new BTEC Introductory Certificate or Diploma in Sport and Leisure. It covers the three core units, the three personal skills units and the four vocational option units for successful completion of this award. The core units provide an introduction to the sport and leisure industries and the skills required to work in these industries. The personal skills units will help you to prepare for work and the vocational optional units offer you more insight into the working world of sport and leisure.

The qualification

If you are working towards the Certificate you will need to successfully complete four units. If you are working towards the Diploma you will need to successfully complete eight units. Each unit consists of 30 or 60 hours of study. Unit 3 (core unit) and all the vocational option units are 60-hour units.

For the **Certificate** you will need to cover:

Core – these are compulsory

   1 Starting work in sport and leisure

   3 The healthy body

Personal skills – choose **one** of these units:

   4 Personal effectiveness

   5 Social responsibility at work

   6 Financial management

Vocational options – choose **one** of these units:

   7 Organising a sport or leisure event

   8 Issues in sport and leisure

   9 Taking part in sport

   10 Introducing customer service

For the **Diploma** you will need to cover:

Core – these are compulsory

   1 Starting work in sport and leisure

   2 Working in sport and leisure

   3 The healthy body

Personal skills – choose **two** of these units:

4 Personal effectiveness

5 Social responsibility at work

6 Financial management

Vocational options – choose **three** of these units:

7 Organising a sport or leisure event

8 Issues in sport and leisure

9 Taking part in sport

10 Introducing customer service

● *Assessment and grading* ●

All units except the personal skills units are graded as pass, merit or distinction. Personal skills units are only graded as a pass.

For the certificate, Unit 1 is externally assessed. For the diploma, Units 1 and 2 are externally assessed. This means you will complete a project set by Edexcel, the awarding body of this qualification. You can complete the project over a period of time, giving you plenty of chances to have your work checked and reviewed by your teaching staff. You can complete the project in a variety of ways, so choose a way which suits your working style the best. Your project will be internally assessed by your centre before being checked by an external BTEC verifier. The remaining units are internally assessed. This means, to pass the unit, you will complete an assignment set and marked by your tutor.

For each unit you must achieve a pass grade to achieve a qualification grade. The qualification is made up of units of 30 and 60 hours of learning. It is the grades awarded for the 60-hour units that will determine your grade for the qualification. For example, if you are taking the Certificate, your grade will be decided by your best performance of the two 60-hour units. If you are taking the Diploma, your grade will be determined by your two best performances in the four 60-hour units.

The personal skills units and externally assessed units don't contribute towards your qualification grade.

● *Putting together your portfolio* ●

Your portfolio is an important document and needs to be put together with a clear structure to it. The evidence that it holds will determine whether you pass or fail, so keep it safe!

Your evidence may come in a variety of formats so your portfolio needs to be able to have in it the following:

- *Subject content, knowledge and understanding and associated skills*
- *Observer (witness) or personal statements*
- *Key skills and wider issues such as moral, spiritual and cultural issues*
- *Work experience*
- *Project reports*
- *Case studies*
- *Results of simulations or activities.*

If you gather evidence for one assignment which may also meet the needs of other learning outcomes you will need to carefully cross-reference the material. You should always remember that quality of material will always be valued above quantity. Your school or college may have a ready-made format, but you should take some tutor guidance on what is best. Make sure you look at the grade descriptors in the Unit so that you can match or target your efforts to achieve the best grade you can. Proper use of appropriate language will help, as will breadth and depth of knowledge in the right places. You may be asked some additional questions too, so be prepared.

Examiners will want to see that your evidence is:

- *Valid (appropriate)*
- *Reliable (consistent with real practice)*
- *Suitable (for the assessment needs).*

Adult literacy, adult numeracy and key skills

The scheme also includes mapping of adult literacy, adult numeracy and Key Skills at level 1. The adult skills are for post-16 candidates only.

The Key Skills are:

- *application of number*
- *communication*
- *information technology*
- *improving own learning and performance*
- *problem solving*
- *working with others.*

Special features in the book

There are a number of features throughout the text to encourage you to think about the sport and leisure industry. They also encourage you to find out information, undertake activities that are relevant to sport and leisure and gather evidence towards your assessment.

Case studies: These are real-life (or simulated) situations involving customers and people working in sport and leisure. The questions that follow each case study give you the opportunity to look at important issues and widen your understanding of the subject.

Give it a go: Issues relevant to sport and leisure are raised for you to discuss or work through either with a partner, in groups or on your own.

*What if?...*These present situations which may arise and provide you with opportunities for problem solving.

Think about it: These are thought-provoking questions about issues or dilemmas that are relevant in sport and leisure. They can be done individually or in groups.

Evidence activity: These are activities that provide you with practice evidence to show that you understand the work required in the unit. By working through the activities you will gain evidence to meet the grading criteria for each unit at pass, merit or distinction grade – or only a pass grade for personal skills units.

Other features included in this book are:

- **Key terms** are picked out and explained where they occur in the text. This helps to make clear any jargon (specialised language) used.
- an end-of-unit **knowledge check** and word search. This allows you to recap on the knowledge you have learnt throughout the unit. You are then asked to find the answers to the questions which are hidden in a word search.

This book has been written by people with experience of the sport and leisure industry who have a commitment to encouraging you to consider a career in the industry. We wish you the best of luck on your course as you begin your journey towards a career in sport and leisure. We hope you find this book stimulating and useful.

Ray Barker, Bob Harris and Louise Sutton

unit 1

Starting work in sport and leisure

In this unit you will discover the wide variety of organisations and work opportunities that the sport and leisure industry offer. You will also learn how the job you choose affects your lifestyle and, of course, how your lifestyle affects the job you choose.

This unit is externally assessed. This means you will complete a project set by Edexcel, the awarding body of this qualification. You can complete the project over a period of time, giving you plenty of chances to have your work checked and reviewed by your teaching staff. You can complete the project in a variety of ways, so choose a way which suits your working style the best. Ask your teacher what to expect from the external assessment.

Throughout this chapter, you will be asked to carry out a variety of activities and exercises that will help you cover these three outcomes and then complete your project.

In this unit you will need to learn about:

- different types of sport and leisure organisations
- different types of jobs that are available to you
- the effect of your lifestyle on any job you choose.

What is sport and leisure?

There are a variety of organisations and therefore jobs in the sport and leisure industry. Before you can think about what sort of job you might like, it is important to understand what the two words 'sport' and 'leisure' mean. Let us start by looking at some of the important ideas and words that you will come across in this unit and the rest of the book.

THINK ABOUT IT

▲ What do all sports have in common?

What is sport?

Sport is described in the Oxford Concise Dictionary as: 'an activity involving physical exertion and skill in which an individual or team competes against each other'.

GIVE IT A GO: sport

1 In small groups, write down some ideas, that you all agree on, that describe sport. Write the words you think are the most important in CAPITAL LETTERS. Be ready to share your ideas with the rest of the class.

2 What did you decide? Did you have any of these words:

   • rules
   • competition
   • fitness
   • skill?

In what ways could you be involved in sport?

- *You could take part in sport yourself – you might play badminton or swim.*
- *You could watch other people play sport – you might support a local football league team.*
- *You might buy sports equipment or clothing, such as trainers or a replica shirt.*
- *You might go on a sporting holiday – like skiing either at home or abroad.*
- *You might coach sport to other people as a swimming teacher or soccer coach.*
- *You might read about sport in newspapers and magazines, watch sport on TV, listen to games on the radio or even follow scores or live updates of games on the Internet.*

What is leisure?

Everybody has leisure time – time set aside for having fun and relaxing. Most towns and cities have leisure centres, colleges offer leisure qualifications and your local council may have a Leisure Services Department. But what is leisure? The Oxford Concise Dictionary describes leisure as: 'time spent in, or free for, relaxation or enjoyment'.

GIVE IT A GO: leisure

1 In pairs write down what the word leisure means to you. Give some examples of leisure activities.
2 When can you take part in leisure activities?
3 List ten activities you like to do for relaxation and enjoyment.
4 Look at this list and see how many people put down a sports-related activity?

Now you have an understanding of the difference between sport and leisure, you should be able to identify places in your local area that provide you and other people with sport and leisure activities.

Different types of sport and leisure organisations

There are many different kinds of sport and leisure organisations. They can vary for different reasons including:

- *type (what services they offer)*
- *structure (how the organisation works, who runs it, etc.)*
- *location (where the organisation is e.g. by the sea or in a city centre).*

Types of organisations

There are many different types of sport and leisure facilities, ranging from sport, leisure and health clubs to visitor attractions, educational establishments and cultural heritage sites. These **providers** are different because they offer different types of services to their customers and each of these facilities is provided by different types of organisations. The type of organisation will depend on its particular aim, for example, a museum or heritage site will aim to educate and entertain customers, while a sports goods retailer will aim to sell its customers quality sports clothing and equipment. These aims affect how each organisation offers its goods and services to you and other customers.

EVIDENCE ACTIVITY

Range of sport and leisure organisations

1 Look at the following spider diagram and try to find places near where you live that fit under each heading. **P3**

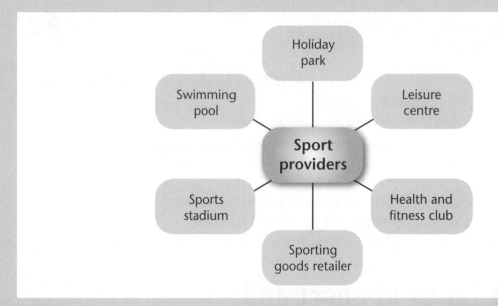

Holiday park

Swimming pool

Leisure centre

Sport providers

Sports stadium

Health and fitness club

Sporting goods retailer

2 Describe what sport and leisure opportunities they offer customers, the types of jobs they offer and where they are generally found. **M2**

3 You now know that leisure involves activities you do for relaxation or enjoyment. Copy out and complete the following table for leisure facilities that are non-sporting. **M2**

Table of leisure facilities and activities

Type of organisation	Local example	What activities do they offer?	What types of jobs are available?
Museum or visitor attraction			
Cinema			
Heritage site (castle or other important building)			
Theatre			
A live music venue			
Caravan or camping park			
School or college with evening classes			
Casino or night club			
Theme park			
Library			

Structure of providers

If you work in the sport or leisure industry, then you will work for one of a group of different organisations. The type of organisation can affect a number of factors in working life.

● *Private providers* ●

Private providers are providers who offer goods and services to make a profit and are often referred to as the **commercial sector**. You will find this type of provider on the high street, for example sports-goods retailers like JJB Sports or Sport Soccer. Since making money is the most important factor, the commercial sector must make sure they are offering goods and services that people like you want, at a price you are prepared to pay.

> **GLOSSARY**
>
> **Commercial sector** is all the organisations that make money from providing goods and services.

GIVE IT A GO: commercial sector

1 In small groups, find out:

   a How many of you are wearing trainers, replica kits or other sports-related clothing?

   b How many different makes, for example Nike, Adidas etc. are there in your class?

   c What price was paid in total for the various items?

2 Draw up a table to show your findings.

GIVE IT A GO: private organisations

For private organisations it is really important that they attract and keep customers. What would happen to Alton Towers if people only went once? They would eventually go out of business. What do you think Alton Towers does to make sure that as many people as possible visit again and again? Look at the following table and decide which ones will help make customers return.

Keeping customers

Situation	Good for keeping customers	Bad for keeping customers
Happy, enthusiastic staff		
A range of rides and activities for all ages		
Litter everywhere		
Good value for money		
Special prices for families, pensioners etc.		
Long queues and lots of waiting		
New rides every two or three years		
Some rides not working most days		
Places to eat and drink		
Rides and activities that are safe to use		

There are different types of private companies that exist, all with the aim of making a profit for their owners.

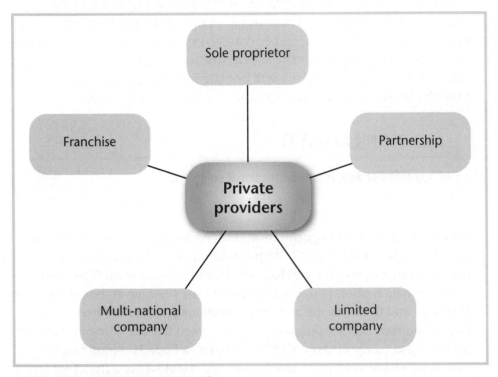

▲ **Different types of private providers**

The first is called a sole proprietor. This is an organisation where the owner works for him or herself and all the money made is his or her own profit. This also means that if the organisation loses money, he or she will have to take responsibility and pay the debts. Personal trainers can be sole proprietors, as could shop owners selling sports equipment.

Another private provider is called a partnership. A partnership is where two or more people set up a business which they run together – they are all the bosses. Sometimes partnerships are necessary because it brings together enough money to start the business, as well as all the necessary skills and experience to run a successful business. Partners will share the profits (or losses) made and share the responsibility of running the business.

Some partnerships can be formed into a limited company. A limited company is similar to a partnership but the key difference is that each person involved is legally responsible for any debts of the organisation. This means debts are paid by each person, but only up to a certain level. This level is based on how much each person **invested** in the organisation. If a business run by a partnership goes wrong then the partners might have to sell their homes, cars or furniture to clear the debts, whereas in a limited company, the owners only lose the money they invested.

GLOSSARY

Invest means to put money towards starting a company, helping it to expand or simply to help it operate.

As an organisation continues to grow it may become a multinational company. This means it offers goods and services in many different countries around the world. Nike is an example of a multinational company. It has offices and factories in many countries, its products are sold in shops around the world and it even sponsors international sports teams like the Springboks – the South African rugby team. There are many reasons why a company will operate in different countries – it may be cheaper to make products abroad, or wages are lower.

THINK ABOUT IT

Can you think of any other multinational companies?

Another type of private organisation is called a franchise. An individual or group buys permission to sell the goods or services of a company and to use that company's name and logo etc. Pizza Hut is a famous food outlet franchise which offers people the chance to use the famous brand name of Pizza Hut and to sell all the associated products and services that go with this. If you want to take on a franchise you need to have a lot of money to invest. It can cost you about £180,000 to start a Pizza Hut franchise! Companies have strict rules and regulations about where a franchise can be opened and how it can be run. A franchise owner can be their own boss, but will still have to operate according to the main company's rules.

• *Public providers* •

A public provider offers a wide range of sport and leisure facilities that are managed by your local council or the government. For example, your local council gym or the children's play area in the local park are run by public providers.

The public sector exists to provide services to everyone in the local area. Their aim is to try to improve people's lives by encouraging lots of people, of all ages and backgrounds, to take part in sport and leisure activities in order to keep fit, healthy and entertained. This also helps prevent people from getting involved in activities that are undesirable such as breaking the law. Unlike the commercial sector these organisations do not aim to make a profit, but they also don't want to lose money!

• *Non-profit organisations* •

Finally there are organisations that are described as non-profit-making. In the private sector, the profits made are shared between the owners and investors of that organisation. An organisation that is non-profit-making puts any money made back into the business to benefit the business. This is known as re-investing and is not the same as losing money.

CASE STUDY – PETERBOROUGH CITY COUNCIL

Peterborough is a large and expanding city in Cambridgeshire and 156,000 thousand people live and work there. Leisure and sport play an important part in making living in Peterborough more enjoyable. A wide range of activities and services are provided for people to use in their spare time. There are two large sports centres, a 25-metre indoor swimming pool, a 50-metre outdoor swimming pool (which opens in the summer months), plus libraries, parks, pitches, playgrounds, classes/courses and other events for local people to enjoy. Prices are kept as low as possible to enable as many people to use the available facilities. Local authorities may also run a variety of schemes and events to encourage people to play sports or take classes. The sporting events are often organised by sport development officers.

a Why do you think Peterborough City Council provides all these facilities?

b What would life be like for local people if they were not there?

c What problems might arise if people did not have these facilities to use?

GIVE IT A GO: non-profit organisations

Look around your neighbourhood. Do you have any of the following:
- associations
- clubs
- societies
- unions
- charities
- universities
- churches?

Make a list of some examples from your local area.

All of the organisations listed in the *Give it a go* activity above can be described as non-profit-making. Any money collected from events, donations, entrance or membership fees for example are used to help the organisation carry out its work. For example, the money might be used to pay for the insurance on the building, buying new sports equipment, designing a new exhibition or paying staff salaries.

Location of providers

Sport and leisure providers plan carefully where they open their organisations. The area in which an organisation is found not only has a strong impact on the kind of service that local people want, but also affects the number of customers available to the organisation.

▲ There is no point in opening a surfing centre in the Alps!

● *Geographical reasons to open a facility* ●

There are **geographical** reasons for choosing a facility's location. Do you want your facility in a city, urban area, rural area or even at the seaside? For example, you can find various kinds of holiday accommodation at different holiday destinations. A seaside resort like Blackpool will have a range of accommodation from large hotels, which may be part of a large group or chain, to individual bed-and-breakfast guest houses, owned by one person, each offering seaside activities or access to sea-life centres. A resort in the Peak District of Derbyshire is more likely to have facilities and activities based around walking, climbing and mountain biking.

● *Regional variations* ●

The history and landscape around facilities also has an effect on the services offered by a facility – giving it a local feeling. For example, the Black Country museum in Birmingham shows life in the Midlands

WHAT if?

...you were running a sport or leisure organisation?

Look at the following list of sport and leisure organisations:

- a diving club
- a sheep-dog training class
- a health and fitness centre
- a cinema.

Where would you want to locate each one? Why?

during Victorian times while a leisure centre in Cornwall could offer surfing lessons. These differences are called regional variations.

Some large organisations such as the Disney Corporation operate sites worldwide – there are Disneyland parks in Florida, Paris and Tokyo. These companies will choose the location based on research into where their products are popular and where they think lots of people would like the service or can afford to pay for the service!

● *Proximity and accessibility* ●

Some companies, such as franchise restaurants, offer the same range of products regardless of the location. The location of an organisation may affect whether you want to work there. For example, you may choose to work in the McDonald's at the end of your road because of its **proximity** to your home. You may choose to work as a lifeguard at the leisure centre in the town next to you because it is on a bus route and so easily **accessible** to you.

> **GLOSSARY**
>
> **Proximity** is how close one thing is to another.
> **Accessible** means easy to get to.

GIVE IT A GO: location of providers

1 With a partner, draw up a table with the following headings:
   - town location
   - seaside location
   - rural location
   - European location
   - international location.
2 Think of a sport or leisure organisation. Discuss what difference there might be when working for this organisation in each of these areas. Think of examples of both positive and negative effects. Be ready to share your thoughts with the rest of the group.

Different types of sport and leisure jobs

You have seen that there are many different types of sport and leisure providers. Within each of these organisations there is also a wide range of jobs. As in any other area of work, there are skills and factors that are common between jobs but there are also factors that are unique to some positions. In this section you will learn to identify the types of jobs in the sports and leisure industry. You will investigate the specific job roles of each position and also what skills or personal requirements are necessary for each job so that you can be successful in your chosen position.

Types of sport and leisure jobs

Just like any other job you might apply for, jobs in the sport and leisure industry vary depending on:

- *the type of job to be done*
- *where the job is based*
- *what the job requires you to do*
- *the level of responsibility the job requires.*

Sport and leisure is a service industry. This means that it is concerned with **non-essential items** like holidays and entertainment.

> ## GLOSSARY
>
> **Non-essential items** are items that are not needed to live. For example, a television is a non-essential item.

WHAT if?

...I went swimming instead of doing the weekly shop?

In small groups, list the differences between going for a swim at your local pool and doing the weekly shopping. Think about what you eventually end up with when you pay for the goods or services, when you might carry out the activity and how essential it is to survival.

You may have decided that you go for a swim in your spare time whereas you carry out the weekly shop during the day. Going for a swim is not an essential activity to most people whereas having food in the house certainly is!

• *Shift jobs* •

Sports and leisure organisations will employ people on a different basis depending on the organisation's requirements and the employee's particular circumstances. Many sport and leisure facilities are open for long periods of the day, seven days a week, for example most major hotels are open 365 days a year and operate 24 hours a day! This often means that you will be required to work in shifts. Working in shifts means you can work different hours during a particular week to ensure that the facility is open for as much time as possible and at times that are convenient for all customers. For example, as a lifeguard at a swimming pool, you may work an early shift one week (which could start at 6am and end at 2pm) and the afternoon or late shift the next week (starting at 2pm and ending at 10pm). In both cases your total working hours are the same. Staff who work on this basis are more likely to be full-time or permanent employees, who work an average of 37–38 hours per week.

● *Part-time jobs* ●

Sports and leisure facilities are not always busy. Your local sports or leisure centre is busiest during the evening and at weekends. At these times, centres will need extra staff to deal with customers and activities and will employ staff only when they are needed. These staff members are often called part-time staff. They will work a limited number of hours based on when the organisation needs additional help and when they are available. Some people, for example parents with young children or students at college, may not be able or want to work full-time. They will earn money based on the number of hours they have worked for the organisation.

● *Temporary jobs* ●

In some cases, a special event might only require staff for a limited period of time. The organisers of a large exhibition like the Motor Show at the NEC in Birmingham will only hire staff for the few days that the show is open. When the show closes the job ends. These staff are temporary staff.

● *Live-in jobs* ●

Some organisations have facilities in a number of places and for those particular jobs, you may have to work away from home.

...you worked at a Butlins holiday resort?

1 Visit the Butlins Holiday website. A link is available at www.heinemann.co.uk/hotlinks (express code 0005P).

2 The website gives you information about Butlins holidays and where you can find a Butlins holiday resort. Look around the website to see what kind of activities are offered. Now think about the kinds of jobs that Butlins could offer you.

From the website you will see that Butlins Holiday villages are situated in a number of coastal locations in England and Wales. They require large numbers of staff to operate the wide range of facilities on each site. Many staff members may live near to the resort, others however could live in other parts of the country and may have to live on site while they are employed by Butlins – these are live-in staff. Advantages of living in might include:

- *accommodation and board provided by the employer (no rent to pay)*
- *no travelling to work*
- *access to the facilities on site during your free time*
- *staff immediately available for cover in an emergency.*

Can you think of any disadvantages of living-in? Be ready to share them with the rest of the class.

CASE STUDY – FULL-TIME, PART-TIME OR TEMPORARY?

Look at the following three case studies and see if you can identify some of the differences between Damion, Diarmaid and Manjula's jobs. In pairs, read the case studies and answer the following questions.

a What type of job is each person currently in – full-time, part-time or temporary?

b Who is in a seasonal job? What does this mean?

c Who do you think works on a shift system? Why?

| Damion is a lifeguard at his local swimming pool. He is currently at college studying for the Edexcel introductory qualification in sport and leisure. He is only available to work during the evening and at weekends and holidays. | Diarmaid has just finished a Sports Science degree at university and is now working as a beach lifeguard near Newquay for the summer. He is currently applying for jobs at leisure centres around the country. | Manjula works at her local sport and recreation centre as a senior lifeguard. After gaining a number of sports qualifications at school and college, she began as a lifeguard three years ago and has just been promoted to her current post. |

• *Freelance or self-employed jobs* •

GLOSSARY

One-off is something that happens once only.

Some people prefer to work for themselves and be their own boss rather than work for someone else. These people are called freelance or self-employed workers. Companies and organisations will often employ free-lance workers to complete a particular **one-off** job for them such as designing a new advert or logo for the company. Many people who have the skills and expertise to work for themselves often prefer the freedom that they get from working for themselves. They can choose when to work and what jobs to take on.

• *Job responsibilities* •

Each job role has a different level of responsibility. There are three main levels:

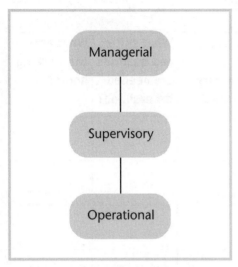

▲ **Three main levels of responsibility**

Operational staff are the staff members who deliver the services or goods – a cinema projectionist or lifeguard. Operational staff are managed by a supervisor who ensures that they are working at the right time and in the right place, ensures everything runs smoothly and that all jobs are done.

Each organisation is looked after by a manager who is ultimately responsible for the running of the organisation or business. This job will require a range of skills, experience and often qualifications, all of which take time to gain. As you gain more work experience, you may be able to progress from being an operational staff member to a supervisor and eventually a manager.

• *Skilled and unskilled jobs* •

Some jobs are termed skilled or unskilled. Skilled jobs generally require special training to do, like a carpenter or plumber. Unskilled jobs do not require specialist training, such as a cleaner at a hotel or a waitress. Skilled workers might earn higher wages because of their special skills. Some skilled jobs may be called craft jobs. These jobs require skills to produce items by hand, for example, a pastry chef who has to make particular desserts or pastries by hand.

EVIDENCE ACTIVITY

Range of jobs

1 Visit your local sport or leisure centre and make a list of all the types of jobs that you can find there. How many of each job are there?

2 Using the information you gathered in **1**, complete the table below. **M1**

Type of Job	Examples	How many are full-time?	How many are part-time?	How many are temporary /seasonal?	What skills and qualities are needed for each job?	What are the working hours?
Operational Staff						
Supervisory staff						
Managerial staff						
Skilled workers						
Unskilled workers						
Freelance workers						

3 Do any of these jobs appeal to you? If yes, write down the job, describe the organisation and say why you think you would like to do that job.

If none of these jobs appeals to you, research other jobs in the sport and leisure industry and choose one that you find interesting. Describe both the job and organisation. **P4**

Job roles

What is a role? The Oxford Concise Dictionary describes a role as: 'a person's function in a certain situation'. A job role is what a person in a particular job is expected to do. A lifeguard, for example, must be ready to save peoples lives if needed. He or she is also expected to watch customers in a pool, give information, enforce the rules of the pool, undertake regular training and have the necessary qualification.

GIVE IT A GO: different job roles

1 Copy and fill in the table below. Be ready to share your answers with the rest of the class. An example has been completed for you.

Role	Sports coach	Receptionist	Café manager
1	Keep records		
2	Check equipment		
3	Be suitably dressed		
4	Instruct people		
5	Provide information		
6	Organise equipment		
7	Keep up to date		
8	Ensure safety		
9	Organise competitions		
10	Promote a good image to others		

WHAT if?

... you worked as a ballet teacher?

Your job role would be to teach certain dance movements and to ensure students have the correct balance, do not injure themselves and are having fun!

Choose three sporting jobs that you are interested in. List all the things that you think a person in that job would have to do.

● *Investigating job roles* ●

When you are choosing a job it is very important to **investigate** the job you are interested in. If you know enough about the job's roles, what will be expected of you, the hours you will be working etc. you will have a much better idea if the job is one that suits you and your lifestyle. Let us look in more detail at some jobs in sport and leisure that you might find interesting.

GLOSSARY

Investigate
means doing careful research so that you know all the facts about something.

CASE STUDY – PONDS FORGE INTERNATIONAL

Investigating job roles

Look at the following case study and try to think of as many different jobs as you can that are needed to manage and run the centre successfully.

▲ **Ponds Forge International Swimming Centre hosting a national swimming competition**

Ponds Forge International Swimming Centre is a nationally important sports facility. The facilities include: a 50-metre 10-lane swimming pool; a leisure pool with a wave machine and water slides; a 6-metre diving pit with a number of diving boards and a night club. It also has a large health and fitness suite and a large sports hall providing badminton, basketball and many other indoor sports. It hosts many local, national and international competitions, many of which are seen on television. The building has large changing rooms, a café, offices for the many administrative and security staff plus a host of other features and facilities. A huge range of activities are offered from exercise classes to discos, to children's parties.

a In small groups, list as many different jobs as you can think of that would be found at Ponds Forge International Swimming Centre. **P1**

b Try to describe what kind of jobs the different people working at Ponds Forge have i.e. is the job full-time or part-time? Link these jobs with the skills, qualifications and qualities you think each person needs. **P2**

c Log onto the Ponds Forge website – a link is available at www.heinemann.co.uk/hotlinks (express code 0005P). Use the links to look at the various facilities available and describe what happens during a typical week at Ponds Forge International Swimming

Centre. Think of the different activities that are available, the different types of customers and the various staff that are needed at any one time. **M1**

d Write a short story about a typical day for one of the jobs that you think you might like to do. What skills and qualities would you need to do the job well? Include the reasons why you think these skills and qualities are important. **D1**

Personal requirements

For every job role there are certain skills and qualities necessary to ensure the job is done properly and well. Some of these skills are practical, like being able to swim if you are a swimming coach. Other requirements are personal qualities such as being friendly and open if you work with people. Personal requirements also mean taking responsibility for your job role, for example, if you are responsible for opening the shops in the morning, then you are required to be on time.

GIVE IT A GO: personal requirements

Try the following exercise. Listed below are a number of different sport and leisure jobs. Next to these jobs is a selection of personal qualities that a job might require.

Job	Personal qualities
Lifeguard	Honest
Fitness instructor	Punctual
Barman/woman	Reliable
Receptionist	Good team person
Manager	Able to work on their own
Sports coach	Able to follow instructions on their own
Box office staff in a theatre	Friendly
Children's entertainer	Good with people
Health suite membership sales person	Good manual skills
Ride operator at a theme park	Good with numbers
	Good communication skills
	Good sense of humour
	Good time management skills

1 With a partner, match the job to the personal qualities required.

2 Copy and fill in the table below. An example has been completed for you.

Job title	Personal qualities required	Examples of why these qualities are needed
Lifeguard	1 Teamwork	Some rescues in a pool can only be done as a team – a spinal injury for example
	2 Punctual	Needed for starting shifts on time / relieving other staff
	3 Good communication skills	Needed for dealing with customers in the pool and to get safety messages across clearly
	4 Good with people	When carrying out duties at poolside – supervising swimmers
	5 Able to follow instructions	On how to perform certain duties
	6 Able to work on their own	On some occasions, low numbers of swimmers might mean a lifeguard is on duty alone

3 Choose a sport and leisure job that interests you and add it to your completed table. You can share your thoughts with the class.

Work and your lifestyle

Lifestyle factors

GLOSSARY

Lifestyle is the way a person lives their life. For example, the way you dress, the things you eat, the way you spend your spare time or what you spend your money on.

If you work out the amount of time in your life you will spend at work you will probably see that most of your time will be spent in a job. That may sound pretty depressing, but if you have chosen a job that suits your **lifestyle** then you are making sure that you enjoy your job – you will then see how most of your time will be having fun, not just working! In the same way that the job you choose will affect your lifestyle, the lifestyle you want will have an impact on the type of job that will appeal to you.

● *What lifestyle is important to me?* ●

Many of the lifestyle choices you make mean that you will need a regular income, for example, you need money to run a car, pay for your mobile phone calls or buy a house. To meet these needs you will need a job that provides a regular income of a certain amount, and to get that income means you will need to have a regular job.

THINK ABOUT IT

What things in life are important to you? Make a list and share them with other students. Did your list include any of the following:
- social commitments
- type of working life desired – part-time, full-time etc.
- building a career
- time for a boyfriend/girlfriend or family
- sporting commitments
- working close to home
- earning lots of money
- working a variety of hours rather than a 9–5 job
- working in an office or outdoors
- working in a team or on your own
- having flexible working conditions?

If having a flexible work schedule is important to you – you need to fetch your grandmother's medicine at 3 o'clock every day – you can get a job where you work flexitime. This means your working hours start and finish when it suits you, as long as you complete an agreed amount of hours per week or month.

One of your goals may be to become the boss of an organisation. To reach this position you may have to work in a number of other jobs to gain the necessary experience. You may also need to gain extra qualifications. Your immediate lifestyle may be affected as you may need to put in extra time and energy, studying at night or taking on extra shifts. It is important to understand that it may mean some lifestyle sacrifices, but it will mean you have the lifestyle you ultimately desire in a few year's time.

Working in the sport and leisure industry may require you to do shift work. It may also require working at weekends and other unsociable times, such as bank holidays etc. These are all issues to think about when choosing your job and long-term career. Are you prepared to work unusual hours? Are you willing to start work at six in the morning so that club swimmers are able to train in the pool? Are you prepared to work until the early hours of the morning, as a waitress or a croupier at a casino, for example?

Making realistic lifestyle choices

For certain people, some jobs may not be suited to their physical type or lifestyle, for example, a ski instructor must not only know how to ski, but must also like spending long hours outdoors in the cold snow. Some jobs might need a particular physical requirement: a security officer at a

▲ **If you like travelling then perhaps a travelling sales person is the job for you**

night club may need to be a certain height and weight to allow them to carry out their duties successfully. A receptionist must be well presented and have skills in areas such as communication and administration.

It is vital that you are realistic about your abilities to cope in your chosen job. This does not mean you should limit your possibilities – you can always learn to ski, but if you hate snow then you are being unrealistic. For all those people who work in sport and leisure, the ability to cope with the stresses of the job is important. Dealing with people can place a great deal of pressure on you at times. When things go wrong, people will complain, sometimes very loudly! If you have made a realistic lifestyle choice then you will be able to find a job that is interesting, fun and that you love.

● *Choosing a job that suits you* ●

We have seen that there is a wide range of jobs available to you in the sport and leisure industry. These jobs come with a variety of responsibilities and will need a range of qualifications, personal qualities and experiences. The lifestyle you wish to lead will make some jobs more or less suitable to you. Issues such as where you live, the type of organisation involved and the structure of that organisation will affect the qualities, skills and attributes that you possess. For example, a sales person for a health club will need to be a good communicator, honest,

GIVE IT A GO: lifestyle factors affecting job choice

1 Consider the jobs in the following table and look at the various factors listed. In small groups, try to agree which factors apply to the different jobs and why.

Factors the job requires:

- physical fitness
- physical attributes, for example height or strength
- qualifications
- personal skills, for example communication or organisational.

2 Copy the table below onto a poster to display on the wall of your class, using the headings given. Can you fill in the blanks? Some boxes have already been filled in.

Job	Job roles	Personal skills	Qualifications	Physical / personal attributes	Physical fitness
Receptionist		Good communication skills			
Gym instructor			NVQ Level 2 in Exercise and Music		
Sports coach			Criminal Records Bureau check completed successfully		
Box office sales person					
Facility manager				Smart appearance	
Actor at a theme park e.g. Mickey Mouse					Must be able to dance for four hours, in full costume

trustworthy and be able to cope with the pressure to achieve sales targets every month!

Any job in the sport and leisure industry will put pressure on your social and private life. You may need to look carefully at a particular job to ensure that your working and private life will go together. It is important that you are clear about what things in life are important to you: a career, a family life, or being able to play your chosen sport.

EVIDENCE ACTIVITY

Jobs and lifestyle

1 Make a list of five jobs from across the sport and leisure industry. Choose jobs that you have not chosen in previous activities. Now list all the lifestyle factors that might affect those job roles.

2 **a** Copy out and complete the following diagram:

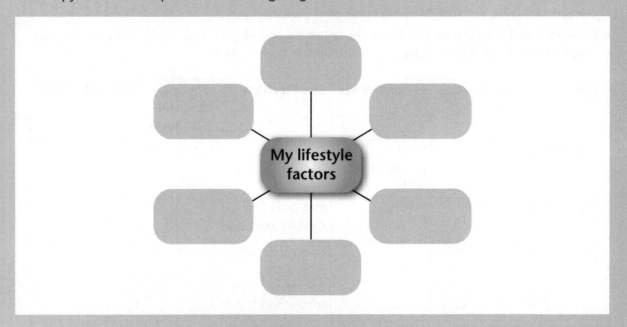

My lifestyle factors

   b Choose two jobs that you are interested in. Using the lifestyle factors you wrote down in **a**, describe how your lifestyle will be influenced by doing these jobs.

3 In pairs, choose two different organisations in the sport and leisure industry that appeal to you. Write a paragraph that explains why working in these two different organisations will affect your lifestyle differently.

Find the answers to the questions in the puzzle. They could be written across, down or diagonally, backwards or forwards.

```
P B U R E G A T I O N S E A S O N A L B D Q J F
A I S G E M A N V L X F Z H E E K T N P H U O T
R C O M N G W T H F R A N C H I S E M E C Y P J
T P C S H I F T S Y S T E M O G I Y R J M G E U
N O I C J H D O J D Q Y R Q P M R K T E A M R W
E A A K C O M U E Z Y U K E L W M D R R O Z A F
R R L Q B S H D E S T G A L J E T E I F O D T K
S G C R K H Y A N C Y X E L V D I Z R U Z B I G
H N O W K T U H W B Z S Z R I W E E Z C X R O N
I S M E E N L E I S U R E U Z F K Z M S I Z N G
P H M I M H F A F R L O S U R E I N E U O A A E
T I I L A R K L C D W L P N L Q M C L C A Z L R
E V T A N J I T R M E E G C U H I A A B Q M Y I
E L M B A A S H H A G M M I B V B Z W T T V M H
T A E M G F U C J N M T K Y R R Q U Z J I L D L
I O N M E G R L C T K N M E P F Z E O E R O C F
O M T E R F E U W E U G S T D R S H I P U W N J
N E S N B R L B O M E W M H B V Y F M Y Q O W S
W X E J K D G E R P F V O L U N T E E R S R P G
T E A M W O R K Q H A I W T I O N F F N X K L C
```

1 _____ is defined as 'time spent on relaxation or enjoyment'.

2 A _____ is a place people go to improve their fitness.

3 A _____ provider is one that exists to make a profit.

4 These people are very important to local sports clubs and organisations.

5 A _____ is a type of private organisation.

6 You are operating a _____ if you use the name, logo and goods of a famous organisation with its permission.

7 Local authorities deliver _____ to local people.

8 _____ is the work system often used in sport and leisure organisations.

9 Jobs that exist at certain times of the year are described as _____.

10 Staff who deliver the product or service are called _____ staff.

11 Your function in a particular situation is known as your _____.

12 Lifeguards in a swimming pool need this skill, as do many other sport and leisure employees.

13 _____ are a lifestyle factor.

14 You can get _____ through your school or college to help you get a job.

15 The person who is in charge is called the _____.

unit 2

Working in sport and leisure

In this unit you will look at what it is like to actually work in the sport and leisure industry through three phases: learning about a job's terms and conditions, the **induction** programme and finally, assessing how well you are performing in your job.

You will learn how to decide which job or career to pursue by finding out all the terms and conditions that apply for any position. This is important so that you, the employee, and your boss, the employer, have exactly the same understanding about what your job role is and how you are to do it. When you first join a sport or leisure organisation you should go through an induction programme, which helps you settle in and become familiar with the processes and procedures of the organisation and other staff. After a period of time at work it is likely that your organisation will want to know how well you are performing, so they will want to assess your performance in some way.

This unit is assessed externally but can be done in 'bite-size chunks'. This means each topic can be tackled as you become more confident and knowledgeable about each stage and the aspect that you need to cover for the assessment. Ask your teacher what to expect from the external assessment.

In this unit you will need to learn about:

- how to consider terms and conditions of different types of jobs
- the induction and training process
- the procedures used to monitor performance.

Terms and conditions of employment

The terms and conditions of a job are all the factors that make up your job contract (or conditions of service), for example, your salary, working hours, what you will need to do, amount of leave, place of work etc. For most people in any kind of work situation the most important factor is how much they will be paid. For some, other factors such as the hours they will have to work, any additional benefits like a pension scheme and what perks there might be in the job (staff discounts etc.) will also be important factors to take into account. In this section you will look at the key factors in detail so that you will have a broader view of some terms and conditions when working in the sport and leisure industry. They are:

- *pay*
- *work patterns*
- *conditions of service*
- *benefits.*

Pay

How much you will get paid is probably going to be your biggest motivator in choosing a job. However, there are two important things to consider:

- *how often you will get paid*
- *how you will get paid.*

> ### GLOSSARY
>
> A **salary** is usually a monthly payment for staff who receive a fixed amount of money per year. **Wages** are usually a weekly payment for workers paid according to the hours worked. These can vary from week to week.

Sport and leisure organisations have different ways of paying **salaries** or **wages** to different types of staff. These are called payment frequencies and methods, and can occur:

- *weekly – as cash or cheque, in a personal envelope or packet*
- *monthly – as a cheque or bank credit transfer (paid straight into your bank account by electronic transfer, also known as BACS).*

• *Rate of pay* •

Managers and supervisors usually earn a salary because they are permanent employees. Hourly, part-time, casual or seasonal staff are usually paid in wages as they may not work a full working week. This is commonly found in the leisure industry with holiday camp staff, activity leaders and staff working at events or shows.

Your rate of pay – hourly, weekly or monthly – has to be confirmed in your contract along with any bonuses you might expect to earn, such as:

▭ *for meeting sales targets*
▭ *end of year/season bonus*
▭ *improving your qualifications.*

▲ **Getting a year-end bonus will be written into your contract**

● *Method of payment* ●

How you will be paid – by BACS, cheque or cash – also needs to be written into your contract so you are clear from the outset. This also means you can budget properly between wage or salary payments.

◯ **THINK ABOUT IT**

> The different payment methods are used for two main reasons:
>   **1** security
>   **2** economy.
> Can you think of any reasons why?

Main terms and conditions of employment

yabla blah blah blah yabla blah blah yabla blah blah yabla blah blah yabla blah blah blah yabla blah blah blah yabla blah blah yabla blah blah blah yabla blah blah
yabla blah blah yabla blah blah blah yabla blah blah blah yabla blah blah blah yabla blah blah yabla blah blah blah yabla blah blah yabla blah blah blah yabla blah blah
yabla blah blah yabla blah blah yabla blah blah yabla blah blah blah yabla blah blah yabla blah blah yabla blah blah yabla blah blah yabla blah blah
blah blah yabla blah blah blah yabla blah blah blah yabla blah blah
blah blah yabla blah blah blah blah yabla blah blah yabla

Benefits

yabla blah blah yabla blah blah yabla blah blah blah yabla blah blah yabla blah blah blah yabla blah blah blah yabla blah blah yabla blah blah
yabla blah blah yabla blah blahyabla yabla blah blah blah yabla blah blah blah yabla blah blah yabla blah blah blah yabla blah blah blah

Normal hours of work

yabla blah blah yabla blah blah yabla blah blah blah yabla blah blah blah yabla blah blah blah yabla blah blah yabla blah blah yabla blah blah
blah blah yabla blah blah yabla blah blahyabla yabla blah blah blah yabla blah blah blah yabla blah blah yabla blah blah blah yabla blah blah blah

Rate of pay

yabla blah blah yabla blah blah blah yabla blah blah blah yabla blah blah blah yabla blah blah yabla blah blah yabla blah blah yabla blah blah
yabla blah blah yabla blah blah blah yabla blah blah yabla blah blah yabla blah blah yabla blah blah yabla blah blah blah yabla blah blah
yabla blah blah yabla blah blah blah yabla blah blah blah yabla blah blah yabla blah blah blah yabla blah blah yabla blah blah yabla blah blah yabla
yabla blah blah yabla blah blah yabla blah blah blah yabla blah blah blah yabla blah blah yabli

Place of work

yabla blah blah yabla blah blah yabla blah blah blah yabla blah blah blah yabla blah blah blah yabla blah blah yabla blah blah yabla blah blah
yabla blah blah yabli blah blah yabla blah blah yabla blah blah blah yabla blah blah blah yabla blah blah blah yabla blah blah yabla blah blah
yabla blah blah yabla blah blah blah yabla blah blah blah yabla blah blah yabla blah blah yabla blah blah yabla blah blah yabla blah blah yabla blah
yabla blah blah yabla blah blah blahyabla yabla blah blah blah yabla blah blah yabla blah blah yabla blah blah blah yabli

Method of payment

yabla yabla blah blah yabla blah blah blah yabla blah blah blah yabla blah blah
yabla blah blah yabla blah blah yabli blah blah yabla blah blah

Notice

yabla blah blah yabla blah blah blah yabli blah blah yabla blah blah yabla blah blah blah yabla blah blah blah yabla blah blah yabla blah blah
blah blah yabla blah blah blah yabla blah blah blah yabla blah blah blah yabla blah blah yabla blah blah blah yabla blah blah yabla

Leave

yabla blah blah yabla blah blah blah yabla blah blah blah yabla blah blah yabla blah blah yabla blah blah blah yabla blah blah yabla blah blah
blah blah yabla blah blah yabla blah blah yabla blah blah blah yabla blah blah blahyabla yabla blah blah yabla blah blah yabla blah blah blah yabla blah blah
blah blah yabla blah blah yabla blah blah blah yabla blah blah blah yabla blah blah blah yabla blah blah yabla blah blah yabla blah blah yabla blah blah

Sickness

yabla blah blahyabla yabla blah blah yabla blah blah yabla blah blah yabla blah blah blah yabla blah blah yabla blah blah yabla blah blah yabla blah
blah yabla blah blah blah yabla blah blah yabla blah blah blah yabla blah blah blah yabla blah blah yabla blah blah yabla blah blah blah
yabla blah blah yabla blah blah yabla blah blah blah yabla blah blah blah yabla blah blah blahyabla yabla blah blah yabla blah blah yabla

▲ **An example of a contract**

GIVE IT A GO: minimum wages

Sarah and Charulata have both applied for part-time bar work to help them pay for their university and college courses. They are both 21 years old and are not sure of the minimum wage they could expect. The bar owner has offered them an hourly rate of £4.55.

Does this seem reasonable to you, or is it below the minimum wage set by the government? Log on to the National Minimum Wage website – a link is available at www.heinemann.co.uk/hotlinks (express code 0005P) to help you find the answer.

Work patterns

The sport and leisure industry works around the clock and is often called a 24/7 environment as it serves people's leisure needs throughout the day and night. Examples of staff working at **unsocial hours** might include hotel room-service staff available to make meals and drinks from 6am in the morning, to staff working in casinos and night clubs until 5am. Your contract should state the hours that you are required to work.

GIVE IT A GO: working hours

There is an upper limit on the hours people can be asked to work, set by the European Union for young people and adults. These are called the Working Time Regulations. For any employees who work flexitime or odd shifts these are agreed on an individual basis.

1 Log onto the Working Time Regulations website – a link is available at www.heinemann.co.uk/hotlinks (express code 0005P), and find out what the Working Time Regulations for the United Kingdom are.

2 Can you think why Working Time Regulations are necessary?

• *Leave entitlement* •

Another issue that must be agreed upon and written into your contract is your **leave entitlement** and when you can take the time off as part of your shift pattern. Remember that a shift working pattern is a popular way for managers to ensure that there are enough staff members on duty to cover all the necessary jobs, at all times. Sometimes managers will pay employees more to work during unsocial hours such as bank holidays or Sundays – this will also need to be agreed upon and written into your contract. Most leave periods (holiday times) for full-time day staff stretch to two or three weeks per year, which are paid holidays. If your contract includes bank holidays, this might bring your total leave entitlement to 28–30 days per year. Standard contracts for full-time staff usually ask you to work 37–40 hours per week.

> **GLOSSARY**
>
> Your **leave entitlement** is the number of days per year you are allowed to take off as paid holidays.

Finally your contract should also say what breaks in your work pattern you can take such as: snack times, lunch, time away from your computer, sickness and leave for personal reasons such as a death in the family or when a baby is born.

Conditions of service

This phrase covers details given in your contract as we have seen, but it may also give you details of any schemes that the company or organisation run for their employees such as:

- *pension rights*
- *health and welfare schemes*
- *health and safety standards and requirements.*

Benefits

Joining a company can have many employment benefits depending on the nature of the organisation – these are often called perks. Perks add value to your job but do not always have a value in terms of money. The list below explains some of the more common benefits you may come across.

1. *Bonuses*. These are paid out for a number of reasons – being loyal, exceeding sales targets or if the company profits are high. Bonuses are often found in seasonal work, for sales representatives or where products are sold (such as sports equipment shops).

2. *Meals on duty* or *lunch vouchers*. You may get free meals while you are working – mostly where there is a catering outlet or canteen on site e.g. hotels or at an event venue. Some private sector sport and leisure providers offer lunch vouchers which give a discount off lunches in the canteen, café or other outlets.

3. *Uniforms*. Not always the most fashionable items to wear, but they save you buying a range of work clothes, may protect you and will make you look more professional and 'part of the team'!

4. *Free transport*. Many employers will offer a free minibus pick up if their venue is off normal bus routes or in the countryside, such as Flamingo Land in North Yorkshire. If staff finish at unsocial hours, taxi transport may be paid for by the company to ensure staff get home safely.

5. *Season ticket loans*. It is sometimes possible to have a season ticket loan to pay for train travel rather than pay for the ticket in one lump sum. Smaller amounts are then deducted from your wages over a number of months until the ticket is paid for.

6. ***Special deals or discounts***. Many clubs, shops, gyms and leisure complexes offer staff discounts (20% off all items) or **freebies** (free entry to a concert or match, or free use of premises for parties). This type of deal adds extra value to the type of job and working conditions. For example, travel agency staff often enjoy free educational trips abroad, 10% off flight costs and sales bonuses for the amount of holidays sold in a month.

When deciding which job will suit you the best there are a number of factors to consider. It is not just how much money you will earn that is important because conditions and benefits will add value to your job. These issues all need to be looked at and thought about as part of the total job package.

GLOSSARY

Special deals or **staff discounts** are when items or services are sold at reduced costs or prices to staff members.
Freebies is a slang term used to describe things you get for free from an employer. These can be part of your conditions of employment e.g. your uniform or pens.

CASE STUDY – TERMS AND CONDITIONS OF EMPLOYMENT

If you got a job working in youth and community recreation with a local authority, you might find the following terms and conditions quite typical. These are the terms and conditions that The Royal Borough of Windsor & Maidenhead offers its staff:

- **Standard hours of Work** – 8.45am to 5.15pm, Monday to Thursday, Friday finishing at 4.45pm (dependent on the needs of the service)

- **Conditions of service** (in line with national agreements):
  - An annual pay award on 1 September
  - 37-hour working week
  - Holiday entitlement of 30 days, rising to 35 after 5 years continuous service

- **Other policies and terms:**
  - Flexible working may be needed
  - Pension scheme

- Car allowances – for mileage, loans and parking
- No smoking policy
- Staff development and training scheme
- Support for further qualifications

1 Why do you think the phrase 'dependent on the needs of the service' is included?

2 How do these terms and conditions compare to those offered by the private sector?

3 Create a chart that maps: hours, pay, skills and qualifications requested and other features of an employment package found in the private sector (for example, as found in *Leisure Opportunities* magazine).

4 How important are criminal record checks and why?

EVIDENCE ACTIVITY

Terms and conditions of employment

Work pattern	Job
Day-time hourly work	Putting green attendant
Evening and late shifts	Football stadium steward
Seasonal	Leisure centre receptionist
Flexitime worker	Swimming pool manager
Casual work (peak times)	Cinema operator

1 The table above shows a range of work patterns and jobs you may come across in the sport and leisure industry. Can you match the work pattern to the employee? **P1**

2 Choose three jobs in the sport and leisure industry that you are interested in. Copy them into your own table and then fill in the other columns. **P1**

Job	Working hours and leave	Payment method and frequency	Benefits

3 With a partner, carry out some research to compare current rates of pay and what holiday time is offered across a range of jobs in the sport and leisure industry. You can use the publication *Leisure Opportunities* which comes out every two weeks or go to their website for more information – a link is available at www.heinemann.co.uk/hotlinks (M1) (express code 0005P).

4 Working with another partner, interview the staff or management at your local sports shops or leisure centres. Ask them what benefits such as discounts, deals and freebies staff are given. Compare your findings and decide which of the jobs give better (M1) benefits. Create a display to show your findings to the rest of the class.

Induction processes

What does induction mean? In everyday terms it means the processes that you go through once you join a new organisation, which help you to familiarise yourself with:

- ▭ *the people you will work with and report to*
- ▭ *health and safety aspects relevant to the job and facility you will work in*
- ▭ *the organisation itself (e.g. procedures, buildings and resources).*

The induction process or period can last from a day to many weeks. The length of induction depends on the type of job, the contract you have and the kind of organisation. Usually a long induction period means the organisation does not want to rush you into a new job and that they have thought about all the different things you need to learn – not only about the job, but about the organisation too. Asking about the length of an organisation's induction programme during an interview can be a good way of helping you decide what job you would like. Let's look in more depth at the things that go into a good induction.

People

During your induction programme you will be introduced to a range of people. In a large company the personnel officer or human resource manager is usually in charge of running induction programmes and introducing you to all the people you will need to know. In smaller organisations this role may be played by your manager or the business owner.

You may meet your:

- *workmates or colleagues – the people you will work with*
- *supervisor or manager – the person you will report to*
- *personnel officer, payroll clerk or health and safety officer – the people who may provide help at work*
- *customers – users and suppliers.*

• *Company policies and rules* •

The human resource manager or your manager will also introduce you to the staff members who are able to explain company policies and rules. They should also be able to give you an induction booklet containing all the relevant company information, such as:

- *Expected standards of behaviour and dress in the workplace.* For example being polite at all times, what you are meant to wear (smart clothes for reception, sporty for the gym or an apron in the kitchen)
- *Sick leave procedures.* Your manager may expect you to phone in the first day you are sick and then bring in a note from the doctor if you are sick for more than three days
- *Arrangements for time off because of a death in the family.* If you need to attend a funeral, compassionate leave may be granted for a few days or up to a week. This may vary depending on if it is a close member of the family who has died.
- *Arranging annual leave.* Some companies use a **rota system** to book leave days to ensure that not everyone takes the same days. You may have to arrange your leave with your colleagues. Sometimes the person who was most recently hired gets the least choice of when to take their leave! For seasonal work you may have to wait until the facility is closed before you can take much leave, other than odd days off, for example at holiday camps.
- *Staff training.* As a new recruit you will need a number of training sessions to learn about the company computer system, following procedures, dealing with paperwork and so on. With good employers this should be an ongoing process.

> **GLOSSARY**
>
> **A Rota system** is a schedule showing the hours staff will work (usually for shift workers).

▲ Staff training is an important part of the induction process

These rules are all based on established practices which you will need to understand to ensure you do your job well. Try to get up to speed as fast as possible, as learning these rules quickly can have a positive effect on your job performance, motivation and your image with other staff members.

Health and safety

An important part of your induction programme is learning about the company's health and safety policies. There a lot of laws which apply to workplace safety in the United Kingdom and Europe. Your induction programme needs to clearly explain all the laws that are relevant to you in your sport and leisure role.

First of all you will need training to learn the basic rules of looking after people on your premises. You have a **duty of care**, which also means that if you spot a problem you have a duty to report it to someone who can sort it out. If you don't and a customer gets hurt then they can open **negligence claims** against you or your employer. Most good organisations will carry out **risk assessments** on their premises regularly to check for any hazards, such as broken tiles or leaky roofs.

WHAT if?

...*some chairs in the cinema you worked in were broken?*

The next movie is starting in ten minutes.

What would you do about it? Who would you tell?

• *Fire regulations* •

You will need to know what to do in the event of a fire. Your induction booklet, your manager or human resource manager will give you all the information you need, such as:

- *sounding the alarm*
- *clearing the building*
- *moving to safe assembly points – the evacuation procedure*
- *checking for missing persons*
- *returning to the building*
- *knowing how to use fire extinguishers to deal with small outbreaks.*

The legislation covering this is called *Fire and Crowd Safety in Sporting Places*.

• *Handling dangerous substances or heavy equipment* •

In your job you may need to work with dangerous or hazardous substances, such as cleaning fluids, pool filtration chemicals and compressed air or gas cylinders. It is vital that you are given training on how to handle, use and store these substances safely.

Very often in the sport and leisure industry you will find that you need to lift and move heavy or awkward equipment such as portable basket-ball stands or trampolines. Depending on your job your induction programme may also train you in the safest ways to carry or move heavy equipment, both on your own or with colleagues. The legislation which covers this is called *Safe Manual Handling*.

GIVE IT A GO: health and safety laws

1 Log onto the Health and Safety Executive website – a link is available at www.heinemann.co.uk/hotlinks (express code 0005P). Look up the *Safe Manual Handling* and *Fire and Crowd Safety in Sporting Places* legislations.

2 With a partner, write down the main points of each legislation and then present them to the rest of your class.

EVIDENCE ACTIVITY

The importance of a health and safety induction

Read the following scenarios and then answer the questions below.

Scenario 1: Some children are having an activity day at your centre. In the lunch break three stray and go into the store room to explore. One of them gets stuck behind some heavy boxes and cuts himself quite badly on a piece of wire. You are first to find him. What do you do?

Scenario 2: You are just making a final check (on your own for the first time), before locking up the store rooms at a leisure centre. The hall next door is full of children in a gymnastics lesson. You smell smoke in the storeroom which has electrical boxes in it. What do you do? There are fire extinguishers on the wall in the hall.

Scenario 3: Your facility has just held a regional table tennis tournament. The duty manager has asked you to start folding the tables up and to wheel them towards the store rooms. You know they are awkward, but it is just possible for one person to fold and store them. Would you make a start?

1   How could these situations be covered during an induction programme?

2   Why is it important to get training on health and safely issues during an induction programme?

Organisational induction

To help you understand an organisation's structure, where you fit into that structure, the organisation's aims, purpose, objectives and operations you need to receive some further induction materials or information. This information may be in your induction booklet or your manager may explain it to you. Typically this might include information on what other departments there are and how they relate to the area where you work. For example, you may work on the shop floor as a sales consultant of a shop. The other departments may include management, buyers, cleaners or administration staff.

It is also useful to know how the organisation is run and who the owners are – is it run by the local authority, a large chain or is it a family-owned business? This can help you understand priorities that are set for you and help you not to feel like a 'small cog in a big wheel'. If you are considering working for a particular organisation for some time, knowing about its structure and the **chain of command** can help you understand which supervisory or managerial positions you might like to work towards.

GLOSSARY

The **chain of command** is the phrase used to describe who manages which staff in an organisation (it can also show who reports to whom and who gives instructions to whom).

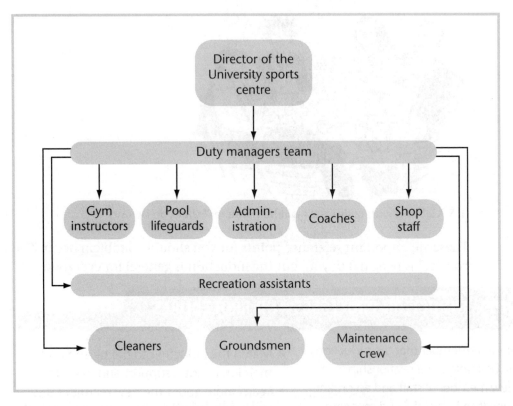

▲ **An example of an organisation's structure**

Knowing the type of the organisation you work for can help you understand the company's working priorities, such as:

- *making a profit e.g. David Lloyd centres*
- *providing a service for the local community e.g. Ryedale council*
- *giving help to youth groups e.g. scouts and guides.*

Induction programmes will also enable you to get **socialised** into the organisation. This means helping you to understand what happens informally in the workplace, for example friendship groups that may have lunch together, social clubs that meet after work or dinners and events that are organised for special occasions such as birthdays or at the end of the year. All these things go together to make you feel as though you belong – a key factor in helping you enjoy your job.

> **GLOSSARY**
>
> To be **socialised** means that you are friendly with other members of staff and fit in with them.

Documents

From the previous sections it should be clear to you that you will receive two key documents very soon after you accept or start a new job:

- *your contract*
- *an induction booklet (or staff handbook).*

▲ Socialising with colleagues will help you feel that you belong

These are important reference points for you should a problem occur. The contract is personal to you, but the induction is general for everyone.

CASE STUDY – INDUCTION PROCESSES AND PROCEDURES

It is important to remember that the induction process is the beginning of a relationship between a new member of staff and an organisation, so it needs to be helpful and meaningful. Research shows that most employees who leave a company are new employees who have not settled in well. It's a challenging period and time is needed for adjustment and learning.

New staff are anxious about how they will get along, follow rules, do a job well and impress the right people. For school and college leavers there may be an additional mixture of emotions and excitement, which needs to be channelled into their work. School leavers may also need some safety guidance as well as extra support if they are shy or have little work experience.

A training design consultancy organisation called DBA offers the following tips on their website:

- Make the most of early enthusiasm – be strong and structured in return.
- Start induction as soon as someone accepts the job – build up their company knowledge.
- Match the induction to the person and their job needs – support and develop.
- Learn more about the new recruit at this stage – use two-way communication to find out what else they can do or want.
- Use induction as a springboard for future development – be informal, but seek further opportunities for development.

You can find out more by visiting the DBA website – a link is available at www.heinemann.co.uk/hotlinks (express code 0005P).

1 What might happen if a new member of staff at a sports shop did not get a good induction?

2 What would be the value of having a 'buddy system' for induction i.e. a person who supports new staff (a mentor) in a leisure centre?

3 Create a checklist of things to mention for an induction at a swimming pool.

4 List three uncertainties a new member of staff might have and three ways to help them with these uncertainties.

WHAT if?

...I am not given an induction booklet?

Create one yourself. Interview other staff members to collect as much information as you can about the company's policies and rules. Type or neatly write them up and place them in a file for you to refer to as often as you like. You could then also show this file to any new recruits who join the organisation after you.

EVIDENCE ACTIVITY

The induction process

1 What do you think the purpose of an induction is? Write a list describing at least ten reasons. **P2**

2 Call in at a local sports/leisure/gym centre and see if they would be willing to give you a copy of their induction booklet or describe their programme to you. If that is not possible ask at your school or college what information new staff are given when they start. In small groups, put together a presentation for the rest of the class that describes your chosen organisation's induction process. **P3**

3 With a partner, think of all the reasons why an induction programme is important to:

   a the organisation

   b the new employee **M2**

4 In pairs, conduct an interview where one person is a night-club owner and the other is a newly hired bar person. As the night-club owner, explain how the induction programme can be used to help the bar person understand their job's terms and conditions. **D1**

Procedures

Company procedures are rules and processes within each job that need to be followed. These can range from looking after customers to looking after yourself.

All sports and leisure organisations have procedures. They are rather like the tendons and ligaments of a body keeping all things in the right place and working well.

In this section you will learn about four important procedures:

- *staff development*
- *appraisal*
- *dealing with disciplinary action*
- *terminating a contract.*

Staff development

Sport and leisure employees need to have a broad range of skills and it is equally important that your employer helps you to develop these. Let's look at a few:

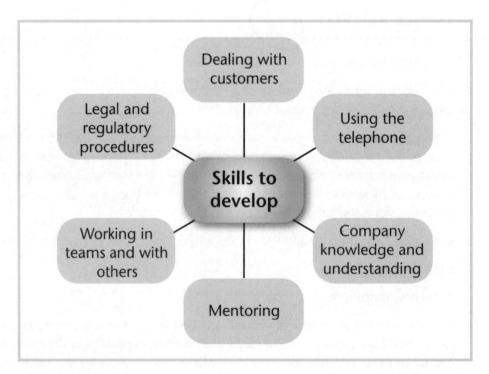

▲ **Developing skills**

● *Dealing with customers* ●

In any sport and leisure job you choose, you will have to deal with a range of customers – young, old, male, female – each with different needs. All these people will want to know many different things about your sport or leisure centre and its activities. You will need to be able to deal with each customer politely and with care – no matter how busy you are! You may not always know the answer to a customer's question, but you must know who in your organisation will be able to help. There are often set procedures for dealing with customer queries such as making bookings, taking fees, checking memberships or giving directions.

You may also have to deal with complaints. Each organisation should have a complaints procedure, which you can follow to help you settle complaints quickly. There may even be a procedure for you to follow if you are receiving abuse from a rude customer!

GIVE IT A GO: dealing with complaints

1 In pairs, visit a local leisure centre such as an ice rink or cinema and ask the staff or management what procedures they have to deal with complaints or angry customers.

2 Again in pairs, role play an angry customer making a complaint and how you, as a staff member, would deal with it.

● *Using the telephone* ●

The way you act or sound when speaking on the phone is called your telephone manner. For many sport and leisure organisations this is very important as a phone call is often the first point of contact a new customer will have with your centre. A polite, responsive reply is important in attracting new members or customers. Each organisation in the industry will have a preferred style or procedure to follow – some may even have a set dialogue that they expect you to use when answering the phone.

● *Knowledge and understanding* ●

You will need to have some staff development time to build up your knowledge and understanding of the facility you work in. This will help you to respond quickly to enquiries without keeping customers waiting. Some examples are knowing:

- *prices of memberships or activities*
- *opening and closing times*
- *special offers or events*
- *where the emergency exits or extinguishers are.*

One procedure for this is to allow you to **shadow** various members of staff for a little time each day or to have a guided tour from an experienced member of staff who can pass on information while you take notes. Some organisations have a weekly meeting where the management pass on information on the week's events, special offers or price changes.

● *Mentoring* ●

This may sound like a complicated word, but it just means that you are given a 'buddy' who is a more experienced staff member who you can call on for advice and guidance. If there are things or situations that you

> **GLOSSARY**
>
> **Shadow** means working closely with a colleague to see how they perform tasks and to learn from them.

don't understand or you have not dealt with before, you can call on your mentor or buddy to help you. He or she will explain how to deal with these situations using the company's procedures. This is a common practice in larger companies in the industry.

• *Working in teams and with others* •

Most centres will have team-based work patterns, whether for daily operations or one-off events.

All types of teams exist in the sport and leisure industry, such as:

- ▭ *professional team players*
- ▭ *professional sports administrators for big clubs*
- ▭ *a team of pool lifeguards*
- ▭ *an event management team at a concert*
- ▭ *staff working as a team in a themed zone of an attraction.*

 THINK ABOUT IT

Team-based working is common in sport and leisure industries.
1 Why do you think it is important to help a new staff member fit in to the team?
2 **a** In a table list five ways you can help a new member of staff feel like a member of the team.
   b In another column, describe why these five points are important to both the organisation and the new staff member.
   c Compare your list with someone else in your class, and together explain how your points can be used to help the new staff member understand their job's terms and conditions.

• *Legal and regulatory procedures* •

You will also have to learn the legal and regulatory procedures laid down by law. These are most likely to include:

- ▭ *health and safety procedures*
- ▭ *data protection procedures*
- ▭ *manual handling procedures*
- ▭ *First Aid and fire procedures.*

(see page 37 for more information on manual handling and fire procedures)

GIVE IT A GO: RIDDOR and COSHH

1 Two important acts that have to be followed are RIDDOR and COSHH. Log onto the HSE website – a link is available at www.heinemann.co.uk/hotlinks (express code 0005P) – and find out what these stand for.

2 Write a short explanation of what each act covers. Be ready to share your answers with the rest of the class.

• *Other procedures* •

Other key areas come into play depending on who your customers are and the nature of the organisation you are working for. You may have procedures for:

- *dealing with children*
- *helping disabled users*
- *serving food*
- *running adventurous activities*
- *selling goods and services.*

▲ **Many organisations have procedures for helping disabled customers**

If you follow all of your company's procedures you are not only working responsibly and safely, you may also be in line for a raise or promotion. However, this usually only happens once you have worked for a set number of months, usually a year, and after an appraisal.

Appraisal

Appraisals are assessment sessions with your boss or supervisor, where your performance and progress are reviewed. Each year, or sometimes every six months, you will be asked to sit down and review what progress you have made within your job. The purpose of an appraisal is to assess the outcomes of your performance against targets set at the last appraisal (or your interview). You can then go on to set **aims** and **objectives** for the next work period. These are usually set with your boss and noted down. These discussions are private, confidential and personal.

▲ Appraisals should be open and relaxed to encourage good understanding

• *Aims, objectives and targets* •

At the start of your job you will have been set aims or made your own objectives or targets. These will be reviewed during your appraisal.

Typical aims for new staff members might be:

- *to work well in the team*
- *to improve a range of work-related skills*
- *to learn a set number of new work-related skills*
- *to complete a problem-free year at work.*

These differ from objectives because they are broader whereas objectives are much more measurable targets.

Typical objectives for new staff members might be:

- *to complete a year with no complaints and no absences*
- *to achieve a promotion to the next grade of pay*
- *to pass a life-guarding award.*

• *Recording documentation* •

Most good sports and leisure providers will have a standard form which will help you prepare for the appraisal session. You will use this form to assess your own performance, to set out your evaluation and write down your new objectives.

WHAT if?

...some staff do not get on well with their managers?

Sometimes staff members and their managers do not get on well. What problems could this cause for the appraisal session? How do you think this negative situation could be dealt with?

EVIDENCE ACTIVITY

Appraisals

Imagine you have just completed your first year as a receptionist at a museum. Your appraisal with your manager is in two days time. Think about the types of aims and objectives you would set.

1 Why do you think it is important to have an appraisal to monitor work? **P4**

2 Describe a procedure for monitoring performance. **P5**

3 With a partner, give examples of how you could assess a staff member's performance using the company's procedures. **M3**

4 Explain why it is important to the manager, staff member and the customers, to review staff performances. **D2**

Compare your ideas with the rest of the class.

Disciplinary procedures

Hopefully you will never go through one of these, but if you do there are some fair guidelines which should be followed.

A **disciplinary hearing** can be called for many reasons some of which are:

- *rudeness to customers*
- *swearing at or abusing other staff*
- *making racist or sexist comments*
- *not following safety procedures*
- *consistently poor job performance.*

Disciplinary procedures should at all times be fair and based on facts, not rumour or just someone's opinion.

If it is a serious matter you might want to seek the guidance of a professional body such as your union, the Hotel and Catering International Managers Association(HCIMA), the Institute of Leisure and Amenity Management (ILAM) or the Institute of Sport and Recreation Management(ISRM). Links to these websites are available at www.heinemann.co.uk/hotlinks (express code 0005P).

You are allowed to have a union representative or trusted colleague to assist you if a disciplinary hearing is called.

• *Grievances* •

These are problems that you raise with the company about matters at work.

You may feel that you have been unfairly treated in some way over a promotion or had something said about you which is untrue. Maybe your terms and conditions vary from someone else's doing the same job.

• *Sources of advice* •

Support is available from a number of independent organisations, such as the Citizens Advice Bureau (CAB) and the Advisory, Conciliation and Arbitration Service (ACAS). The CAB service 'helps people resolve their legal, money and other problems by providing free information and advice from over 3,200 locations, and by influencing policymakers' (taken from the CAB website) and ACAS 'aims to improve organisations and working life through better employment relations. We provide up-to-date information, independent advice, high quality training and we work with employers and employees to solve problems and improve performance'. Links to these websites are available at www.heinemann.co.uk/hotlinks (express code 0005P).

Termination

Termination of your contract may be the result of a disciplinary hearing or a grievance against you, or just through consistent poor performance. This is also known as a **dismissal** or being sacked. This is quite a serious situation as it might prove difficult to get another job and you will no longer have a regular income. New employers will often ask why you left your last job and will need a reference from your last employer – you don't want to leave under these circumstances! At some organisations if you have broken a rule you could be dismissed immediately, but usually you will be given a **notice period**.

▲ **If you have broken a rule you could be dismissed immediately**

● *Redundancy and restructuring* ●

Termination might also mean that your present role is no longer needed and you are going to be transferred to another department or section. For example, if a local authority's old swimming pool is shut down you might be transferred to another part of the organisation, like the sports centre. This might be called job **restructuring.**

Being made **redundant** means that an organisation no longer needs a certain job role. You are then paid to finish with an organisation.

If you could not be found a new position when the pool was closed you might be made **redundant** – this is more serious. There are certain procedures which must be followed before someone is made redundant:

- *staff members must be told that there is a chance that people could be made redundant in the future*
- *the organisation might ask which staff are willing to take early retirement to help ease the process*
- *the management may look at all the skills in the organisation and decide which skills are necessary to keep, and which staff have those skills*
- *they might choose a last in, first out (LIFO) policy.*

If you are made redundant you are usually paid compensation. The amount you will get depends on how long you have worked for the organisation.

GLOSSARY

Unfair dismissal is when someone loses their job but the circumstances are unfair on them e.g. a pregnant woman being asked to leave her job permanently.

If you feel you have been **dismissed unfairly** you may take your case to an industrial tribunal who will make a fair decision about your case. An industrial tribunal is a set of people put together by the government. It helps resolve disagreements between staff members and organisations. Have a look at the Employment Tribunals website for more information – a link is available at www.heinemann.co.uk/hotlinks (express code 0005P).

Going to an industrial or employment tribunal could result in you:

- *being re-employed at the same organisation*
- *receiving compensation, usually money.*

GLOSSARY

Resignation is when you decide to leave an organisation of your own will. This will need to be done in writing.

● *Resignation* ●

If you decide that you no longer want to work for an organisation, maybe you have found a better job, you will need to write a letter of **resignation**. You will need to give this letter to your manager or supervisor within the required amount of notice (this is agreed in your contract). It is a good idea to thank your employer as you may need a reference from him or her in the future.

GLOSSARY

Your **record of performance** is a file or note kept on how well you work and what you have achieved in your job (this can be positive and negative information).

Most organisations will keep a **record of your performance** and achievements while with them, which often forms the basis of your reference. Under the Data Protection and Information Acts you have rights to see that information and ask to have it changed if it is not correct.

GIVE IT A GO: letters of resignation

Working on your own, try to write a letter of resignation. In it you need to explain that you have found a new job closer to home, with better pay and conditions. You will also need to thank your present employer. Compare your letters with those of the rest of the class and ask your tutor to decide whose letter is the most appropriate.

GIVE IT A GO: company procedures

Working with a partner, design some questions you could ask of people in work so that you can describe:

- what staff development opportunities they have
- how performance is monitored and appraised
- what their organisation's policy is on disciplining people and how they can air a grievance
- how their company goes about dismissing people
- what records are kept on staff.

Find the answers to the questions in the puzzle. They could be written across, down or diagonally, backwards or forwards.

1 Terms and conditions of employment are written out in this.

2 Some European laws control the amount of hours we can work.

3 Another word for working benefits or extras you might enjoy as part of your terms and conditions.

4 The process of being familiarised with an organisation.

5 You can be accused of this if you don't take care of customers and there is an accident.

6 You carry out a risk assessment to identify these.

7 What is the name of the Act that prevents employees from revealing your personal information?

8 Setting targets with your boss is usually done at one of these.

9 If an employee makes a complaint against another this is called a . . ?

10 Being 'paid off' when your job no longer exists is called . .?

unit 3

The healthy body

In this unit you will gain an understanding of how your body is constructed and works. You will be introduced to concepts such as **health**, **fitness**, **nutrition** and **exercise**. You will find out what these concepts mean and how they work together to create a healthy lifestyle. You will also learn about lifestyle programming and how it is used to help different individuals develop a healthy lifestyle.

This unit is internally assessed. This means, to pass this unit, you will need to complete an assignment set and marked by your tutor.

In this unit you will need to learn about:

- major muscles, the skeleton, the heart and the respiratory system
- the relationship between sport, leisure and health-related issues
- lifestyle programmes.

Body systems

All your body systems work together to maintain your health and fitness. There are 11 body systems in all. In this unit we are going to focus on the structure and role of four of these systems: the skeletal, muscular, circulatory and respiratory systems.

What does each system do?

System	What is it?	What does it do?
Skeletal system	All the bones in your body and the way they are held together	Your bones are the base of your body; they are what keep you upright. They also provide places for your muscles to 'hold' onto, or attach
Muscular system	All the muscles in your body and the way they work together	Your muscles pull on the bones of your skeletal system to make them move. They are attached to your bones by **tendons**
Cardiovascular system	Your body's blood system and the way it flows through your body	The cardiovascular system carries food and oxygen around your body in your blood and picks up waste for removal
Respiratory system	The way air moves through your lungs when you breathe	The respiratory system takes in oxygen. Oxygen is a vital part of making the energy that keeps you alive and active

Your skeleton

Your muscular and skeletal systems work together to support your body and bring about movement. Your skeletal system forms the bony supportive framework, whilst your muscles form the fleshy part. Your skeleton is made up of bones and cartilage. It is held together at joints. The picture opposite shows the main bones of your body.

Your skeleton consists of 206 bones. It can be divided into two parts – the axial (or the core) and appendicular (or the limbs) skeleton.

The axial skeleton forms the main axis (or core) of your skeleton and consists of your:

- *cranium (skull)*
- *vertebral column or vertebrae (spine)*
- *sternum (breast bone)*
- *ribs.*

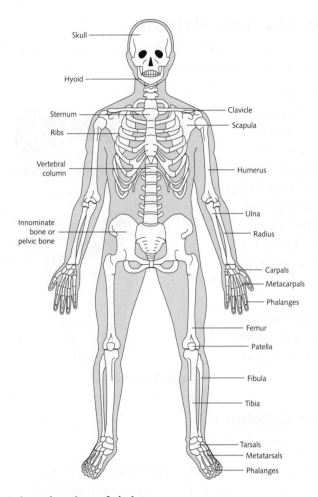

Labels on the diagram:
Skull
Hyoid
Sternum
Ribs
Vertebral column
Innominate bone or pelvic bone
Clavicle
Scapula
Humerus
Ulna
Radius
Carpals
Metacarpals
Phalanges
Femur
Patella
Fibula
Tibia
Tarsals
Metatarsals
Phalanges

▲ **Anterior view of skeleton**

The appendicular skeleton refers to your limbs and consists of your:

▭ *shoulder girdle*
▭ *upper limb bones – arms*
▭ *pelvic girdle*
▭ *lower limb bones – legs.*

Upper limb bones – arms	**Lower limb bones – legs**
humerus (upper arm bone)	femur (thigh bone)
radius (thicker forearm bone)	patella (knee cap)
ulna (thinner forearm bone)	tibia (thicker lower leg bone)
carpals (wrist bones)	fibula (thinner lower leg bone)
metacarpals (palm bones)	tarsals (ankle bones)
phalanges (finger bones)	metatarsals (foot bones)
	phalanges (toe bones)

▲ **Bones of the upper and lower limbs**

• *Types of bone found in your skeleton* •

The bones of your skeleton are given names according to their shape and size. They are divided into the following four categories:

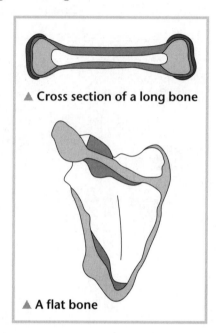

▲ Cross section of a long bone

▲ A flat bone

- ▭ *long bones: these are found in your limbs, such as the femur in your thigh and humerus in your upper arm. They have a hollow centre and two expanded ends.*
- ▭ *short bones: these are small, light and strong, such as the carpals of your wrists and tarsals of your feet.*
- ▭ *flat bones: these are thin and have a large surface area, such as the bones of your pelvis, shoulder girdle and cranium.*
- ▭ *irregular bones: these are the bones that do not fit into the other three groups, such as the vertebrae of your spine.*

• *Functions of your skeleton* •

Your skeleton has five main functions.

1 **Shape and support:** your skeleton gives your body shape and provides the supporting framework that prevents your body from collapsing in a heap on the floor.

2 **Movement:** produced by your joints and muscles working together with your bones for your muscles to pull on.

3 **Protection:** the bony framework of certain parts of your skeleton protects your delicate organs from damage. For example, your brain is protected by your skull and your heart and lungs are protected by your rib cage.

4 **Storage:** your bones store the minerals calcium and phosphorus.

5 **Blood:** some of the long bones of your skeleton (such as your femur and ribs) are responsible for the production of red and white blood cells.

GLOSSARY

Ligaments attach bone to bone.

• *Your joints* •

Joints are where your bones meet and 'join' together. Sometimes bones are attached to other bones by **ligaments**. There are three main types of joint classified according to the degree of movement they allow:

1 **Fixed or immovable joints:** the bones of your fixed joints fit tightly together and are held firm by tissue, such as the bones in your skull.

2 **Slightly movable joints:** at this type of joint your bones allow a little bit of movement, such as the movement between your vertebrae or spine.

3 **Freely movable joints:** these joints allow the highest degree of movement between your bones. They are also called synovial joints. You have six different types of freely movable joint in your skeleton – they are the most common form of joint.

Your muscles

Every movement your body makes depends on your muscles. Your muscles move body parts or your whole body by shortening or contracting. Muscles also help you to maintain your posture and they produce heat.

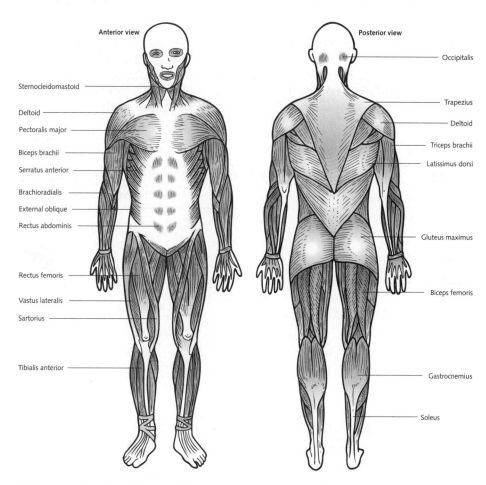

Anterior view

Posterior view

Sternocleidomastoid

Deltoid

Pectoralis major

Biceps brachii

Serratus anterior

Brachioradialis

External oblique

Rectus abdominis

Rectus femoris

Vastus lateralis

Sartorius

Tibialis anterior

Occipitalis

Trapezius

Deltoid

Triceps brachii

Latissimus dorsi

Gluteus maximus

Biceps femoris

Gastrocnemius

Soleus

▲ **The muscular system**

• *Your main muscles and their actions* •

Muscle	Where is it found?	What does it do?
Biceps	Front of upper arm	Bends your arm at your elbow
Deltoids	Shoulder	Raises your arms forward, backward and sideways
Erector Spinae	Lower back	Extends your spine
Gastrocnemius	Back of lower leg	Flexes your knee and points your foot downwards
Gluteals	Bottom	Moves your hip joint
Hamstrings	Back of thigh	Bends your knee joint to bend your leg
Latissimus Dorsi	Middle of the back	Pulls your arms down from your shoulders
Pectoralis Major	Upper chest	Raises your arms at your shoulders
Quadriceps	Front of thigh	Extends your knee joint to straighten your leg
Rectus Abdominis	Abdomen	Supports your abdominal organs and flexes your trunk
Trapezius	Upper back	Rotates your shoulders
Triceps	Back of upper arm	Straightens your arm at your elbow

GIVE IT A GO: muscles and exercise

What muscles are used during the following exercises:

- press ups
- sit ups
- squats?

Your cardiovascular system

Your heart, blood vessels and blood make up your cardiovascular system. This system is the transport system of your body. It transports food, oxygen and a range of other substances around your body. Oxygen is transported from your lungs to your body tissues, whilst carbon dioxide is carried from your cells to the lungs for removal. Life-sustaining nutrients obtained from the food you eat are transported by your blood from your intestines to your liver and body cells. Waste products from the tissues are transported mostly to the kidneys. Your protective white blood cells, antibodies, hormones and even drugs and medicines are also transported in your blood.

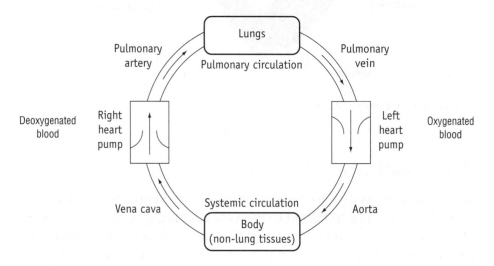

▲ **Double circulation of blood through the heart**

• *Your heart* •

Your heart is a hollow organ situated in the left-hand side of your chest beneath your breast bone. It is made from muscle and moves your blood into and through your arteries, to take blood to your tissues and working muscles. Your heart works as a double pump. The right side of your heart pumps blood to your lungs to pick up oxygen, and the left side of your heart pumps this **oxygenated** blood to the rest of your body. The aorta is the largest artery in your body and carries your blood away from your heart. The vena cava is the largest vein in your body and carries your blood back to your heart. The pulmonary artery is the only artery in your body that carries deoxygenated blood to the lungs.

GLOSSARY

Oxygenated means containing oxygen.

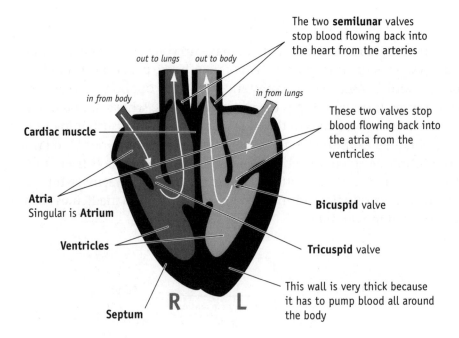

The two **semilunar** valves stop blood flowing back into the heart from the arteries

out to lungs   *out to body*

in from body   *in from lungs*

These two valves stop blood flowing back into the atria from the ventricles

Cardiac muscle

Atria
Singular is **Atrium**

Bicuspid valve

Ventricles

Tricuspid valve

This wall is very thick because it has to pump blood all around the body

R   L

Septum

▲ **The heart is a very hard-working muscle**

Your respiratory system

Your respiratory system is made up of your nose, lungs and breathing tubes. Its function is to take in oxygen for your body's cells and to get rid of carbon dioxide. You breathe air in through your nose. Here the air is cleaned by tiny hairs before it moves into your throat. It then continues its journey down the trachea, also known as your windpipe, into your lungs. This is where the oxygen is taken into your body and where carbon dioxide is taken out.

Oxygen is vital for every cell in your body to work. The amount of oxygen needed to help your cells work changes with the amount of activity you do. During sleep your body needs a lot less oxygen than when you are doing strenuous exercise, such as for running, playing football or riding a bike.

THINK ABOUT IT

How do your body systems work together to move your body during physical activity and exercise?

GIVE IT A GO: the effect of exercise on your body

For this activity you'll need to find an open space in which you can run or walk. You could also use a sports hall or fitness facility with a treadmill.

Before you start:

1 Calculate your maximum heart rate using the formula 220 minus your age.

2 Take your pulse and calculate your heart rate at rest in beats per minute.

Then:

3 Walk for 2–3 minutes. Remain standing and immediately take your pulse using a 10-second count and times by six to give your beats per minute. Record your reading.

4 Increase your pace to a jog for 2–3 minutes or as long as you can sustain your chosen pace. Remain standing and immediately take your pulse using a 10-second count and times by six. Record your reading.

5 Increase your pace to a run for 2–3 minutes or as long as you can sustain your chosen pace. Remain standing and immediately take your pulse using a 10-second count and times by six to give your beats per minute. Record your reading.

6 Take 5–10 minutes to do a thorough warm down and then think about the way your body changed during all the above activities. Write down your thoughts.

EVIDENCE ACTIVITY

Body systems

1 Make a poster or leaflet that describes the structure and functions of the skeletal, muscular, respiratory and cardiovascular systems. To assist you in this task you may find it useful to search the Internet and relevant textbooks for suitable resources.

2 Explain the role of the skeleton, major muscles, the heart and respiratory system.

Health-related issues

Nutrition and diet

The food you eat is broken down by your digestive system and used to provide your body with energy and the building materials it requires to grow and repair itself. You must eat a **balanced**, varied and **healthy** diet to supply all the essential **nutrients** your body requires to perform these functions and remain in good health. There are seven essential nutrients in a healthy diet.

GLOSSARY

Nutrients are chemicals found in food that are necessary for good health.

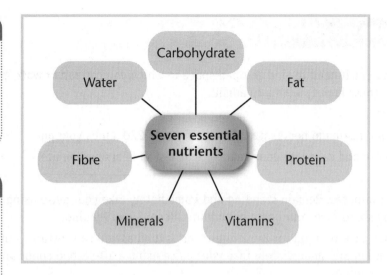

▲ The seven essential nutrients of a healthy diet

The body needs relatively large amounts of carbohydrates, fats and proteins – these are the energy-providing nutrients in your diet. You need much smaller amounts of vitamins and minerals in your diet to keep healthy. Fibre is important for the proper functioning of your digestive tract and helps protect against many diseases, such as heart disease and cancer. Water is one of the most important nutrients required by your body.

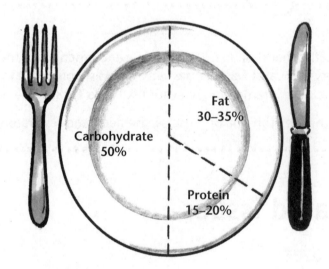

▲ Is your diet a balanced one?

● *Carbohydrates* ●

Carbohydrates provide your body with a quick source of energy. They are found in sugary and starchy foods such as bread, rice, potatoes, pasta, yams, cereals, pulses, root vegetables, sweets, honey and jam. For every gram of carbohydrate you consume you get four **calories** of energy. Current healthy eating recommendations suggest you should eat around 50 percent of your total daily calories from carbohydrate, focusing on the starchy sources to provide the bulk of this.

● *Fats* ●

Fats are your body's second source of energy. There are two main types of fat – saturated and unsaturated – that come from plants and animals. Fats provide nine calories per gram; more than twice as much as carbohydrates. As well as providing energy, fats also protect your vital organs, provide your body with **insulation** and transport some types of vitamins.

Eating too many fatty foods has been linked to an increased risk of certain diseases, particularly heart disease and cancer. Healthy eating recommendations suggest you eat no more than 30–35 percent of your total daily calories as fat, and to cut back on your intake of saturated fat.

Saturated	Unsaturated
full-fat dairy products, butter, hard margarine, lard, dripping, suet, fatty meat, meat pies, paté, cream, cakes, biscuits, chocolate, coconut, coconut oil	olive oil, olive oil spreads, rapeseed oil, corn oil, peanuts, peanut butter, peanut oil, soft margarine, low-fat spreads labelled high in polyunsaturated fats, sunflower oil, safflower oil, soya oil, oily fish, nuts

▲ Types of fat in your diet

● *Protein* ●

Protein is used by your body for growth and tissue repair. It can also be used as an energy source if your body runs out of fat and carbohydrate. Your body does not store protein, so you can eat some everyday. You obtain protein from plants and animals. Every gram of protein you eat provides four calories of energy. To meet healthy eating recommendations your protein intake should be between 15–20 percent of your total daily calorie intake.

Animal	Plant
meat, poultry, fish, eggs, milk, cheese, yoghurt	cereals, bread, rice, pasta, noodles, pulses, peas, beans, lentils, nuts, seeds

▲ Types of protein in your diet

● *Vitamins and minerals* ●

In addition to protein, fat and carbohydrate there are more than thirty different vitamins and minerals you need to remain in good health. If you do not get enough of these nutrients you could develop certain **deficiency disorders**. However, if you eat a good variety of foods and meet your energy needs, it is unlikely that your diet will be short of these vital nutrients.

Vitamins

Vitamins are categorised as:

▭ *fat soluble – vitamins A, D, E and K*
▭ *water soluble – vitamins B, of which there are several, and C.*

Fat-soluble vitamins can be stored by your body, whereas water-soluble vitamins are passed out of your body in your urine. Most vitamins needed to keep you healthy cannot be made by your body and must be supplied by diet. The only vitamins that your body can make are vitamins D and K. Although vitamins do not provide energy they play an essential role in helping your body turn fats, carbohydrates and protein into energy. Vitamins also help your body grow and keep your **immune system** functioning healthily.

Minerals

Minerals are also vital, non-calorie-providing nutrients that are essential to life. Like vitamins they help your body work properly. They are also required in small amounts. Minerals are classified into two groups according to how much of each your body needs:

▭ *macro-minerals: required in relatively large amounts, for example calcium, sodium and potassium*
▭ *trace elements: required in much smaller quantities, for example copper and selenium.*

● *Water* ●

Your body cannot survive more than a few days without water. Water carries nutrients, waste products and internal secretions around your body. It also plays a vital role in temperature regulation, particularly during exercise and helps moves food through your digestive system. It makes up around 50–60 percent of your total body weight.

You lose water from your body through your urine, faeces, evaporation from your skin and when you breathe out air. If you lose a lot of water your body will become **dehydrated**. If you don't do any exercise your body needs about 2 to 2.5 litres of water per day – this is about 6–8 cups – but it will need more if you do heavy work or exercise. The table on page 66 shows how much water goes into and out of a body in one day.

GLOSSARY

A **deficiency disorder** results from a lack of one or more essential nutrients.

GLOSSARY

The **immune system** is the complex system that protects the body from illness and disease.

GLOSSARY

Dehydrated is when your body does not contain enough water.

Vitamin/mineral	Where do you find it?	Why do you need it?	Deficiency disorders
Vitamin A	dairy products, oily fish, liver, brightly coloured vegetables	good vision and healthy skin	night blindness
Vitamin B complex	dairy products, whole grains, lean meat, pulses, vegetables, yeast extract	for making energy, for making red blood cells	anaemia, irritability, fatigue, skin conditions
Vitamin C	citrus and soft fruits, green leafy vegetables, fruit juices, peppers, potatoes	healthy skin and gums, wound healing, iron absorption	scurvy, bleeding gums
Vitamin D	dairy products, oily fish, cereals	increases calcium absorption promoting the growth of bones	brittle bones, rickets
Vitamin E	vegetable oils, whole-grain breads and cereals	protects against heart disease and cancer	deficiency is rare
Vitamin K	green leafy vegetables	helps blood clotting	increases risk of bleeding inside the body
Calcium	dairy products, green leafy vegetables, dried fruit, pulses, white bread and fish with bones	strong bones and teeth, muscle contraction	weak bones
Iron	liver, red meat, green leafy vegetables, fortified breakfast cereals, pulses	for making red blood cells, transport of oxygen	anaemia, fatigue
Potassium	fruit, vegetables, milk, cereals, coffee	muscle contraction	high blood pressure
Sodium	salt, cheese, processed and ready-prepared foods, savoury snacks	fluid balance	deficiency is rare
Zinc	meat, fish, eggs, dairy products, green vegetables, wholegrain cereal	wound healing, better immune system	poor appetite, worse immune system

▲ **Important vitamins and minerals**

Daily water input		Daily water output	
Source	ml	Source	ml
Water	1,200	Urine	1,250
Food	1,000	Faeces	100
Metabolism	350	Skin	850
		Lungs	350
TOTAL	2,550	TOTAL	2,550

▲ Daily water balance for a 70kg inactive adult male

• Fibre •

Fibres is found in plant foods. It helps with digestion, clearing your gut and to prevent constipation. It also helps to control your blood glucose and cholesterol.

◯ THINK ABOUT IT

Some scientists think that most of the population need to increase their fibre intake by a third to 18g per day. Look at your own diet. What kind of foods would you need to eat to increase your fibre intake?

• Supplements •

The vitamin and mineral supplement industry is worth millions of pounds. With the large amount of products available, it is easy to see why you might be tempted to try them in the hope that they might boost your health. However, in general it is thought that if you eat a well-balanced and varied diet, your body will receive enough of the vitamins and minerals it needs. Also, taking large amounts of some vitamins and minerals, such as vitamin A, can actually be harmful to your health.

GIVE IT A GO: factors affecting diet

List all the factors that could affect your food intake and choice.

How might these factors affect your ability to follow a healthy diet?

Awareness of these factors will help you to create realistic and achievable diet plans for your assessment.

• *Relationship between nutrition and sport* •

Good nutrition will allow you to train consistently and effectively. To achieve steady improvements in performance, you must ensure that your diet consistently meets the demands placed on your body by training and competition. Healthy eating and balance of good health principles should be used to plan your meals.

You should eat enough carbohydrates and start refuelling soon after training when your muscle capacity for refuelling is at its greatest. This may mean that you need to eat more often, and you may have to plan your meals according to your training schedule and not fixed meal times. In addition, you should always carry snacks and drinks in your kit bag and make sure that you drink plenty of fluids. It is also important to have rest days to allow your body to recover from the stresses of training and competition.

Fitness

Health-related fitness is your body's ability to cope with the demands of daily life. Fitness is made up of several parts. You need to be a little bit fit in each part to cope with everyday living with ease. Athletes need higher levels of fitness for each part and different sports will require you to develop particular parts more than others to be fit enough to take part in them.

• *Skill-related fitness* •

Different sports also require you to develop different parts of your body as well as requiring different skills. This is often referred to as skill-related fitness or specific fitness. For example, to be a successful tennis player requires good co-ordination, whereas a sprinter needs to have a fast reaction time.

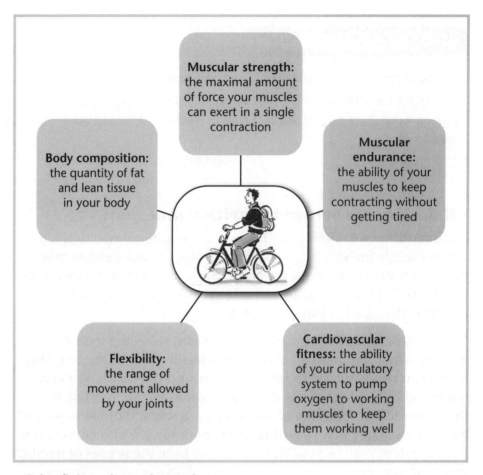

▲ **Being fit is made up of many factors**

The following are all skill-related aspects of fitness:

Speed: the ability to move your body or body parts quickly

Power: the ability of your body to use force at speed

Co-ordination: the ability to move your body and limbs in the correct order

Reaction time: the time taken to react e.g. to the starter gun in a 100-metre race

Balance: the ability to hold your body in a position without falling over

Agility: the ability to move your body into new positions quickly and correctly

• *Training for fitness* •

When trying to get fit you need the correct amount of exercise to make sure that you are healthy and not doing too much or too little. Your fitness training must take into account why you want to be fit and what fitness goals you have. It must also be realistic – that means you should choose a form of exercise that you enjoy, at times that are convenient for you and do it for long enough to make you tired but not so you are exhausted. You also need to carry on exercising for the effects to be maintained. These ideas are also known as the FITT principles of training:

- ▭ *F – frequency refers to the number of times a week you do the exercise*
- ▭ *I – intensity refers to how hard you exercise*
- ▭ *T – time refers to how long you carry out the activity*
- ▭ *T – type refers to the mode of exercise you undertake.*

GIVE IT A GO: fitness training

1 Visit your local health club or leisure centre to look at the range of fitness equipment available.
2 Draw up a chart of your research to include information on the type of equipment available and the muscle groups they work.

Factors affecting your fitness

There are a number of factors that will have an effect on how fit you are, how fit you can become and how long you stay fit.

● *Diet* ●

Healthy eating means choosing the right foods in the right balance, so that you get all the essential nutrients and energy needed by your body to stay healthy. Healthy eating reduces the risk of chronic disease such as heart disease, obesity, diabetes and cancer. Healthy eating will also help you perform better in sports activities.

- eat the correct amount to maintain a healthy body weight
- cut back on your fat intake, particularly from saturated sources
- eat plenty of foods with a high starch and fibre content
- don't eat sugary foods too often
- use salt sparingly and don't eat too much fast food
- ensure adequate intakes of vitamins and minerals by eating a wide variety of foods
- if you drink alcohol, keep within sensible limits
- enjoy your food and don't become obsessed with your diet or dieting.

▲ **A simple guide to healthy eating**

The Balance of Good Health Model is the UK's National Food Guide. It was written by the Health Education Authority as an easy way of helping you to understand healthy eating. The model shows you the types and proportions of food groups you need to achieve a healthy, balanced and varied diet. The model is divided into five food groups: carbohydrates; fruit and vegetables; dairy products; meat, fish or alternate sources of proteins, fats and sugars.

The food group that has a larger slice of the plate should feature in larger proportions in your diet. The food groups with the smallest slice should be eaten in much smaller proportions, especially food with a high fat and sugar content.

▲ A balanced diet

...you were asked to give a talk about healthy eating?

Imagine that you have been asked to talk to a group of school children about healthy eating. Where would you start? What would you include?

● *Alcohol* ●

The current safe limits recommended for drinking alcohol are up to 3–4 units per day for men and for women up to 2–3 units per day. It is also advised to spread alcohol intake throughout the week, to avoid binges, and include two or three alcohol-free days each week.

CASE STUDY – SASHA

Sasha is a 28-year-old housewife with two young children, aged 4 years and 9 months. She has not taken part in any regular exercise since she was pregnant with her second child. She is approximately one stone overweight and has a diet as follows:

1 Keeping in mind healthy eating principles, what changes to her diet would you suggest to help her to lose weight?

2 Write a diet plan for Sasha, taking into account your suggestions from **1**. You can use the same headings from the table.

Breakfast	cornflakes with full-cream milk and sugar
	two slices of toast with butter
	coffee with milk and two sugars
Mid-morning	coffee with milk and two sugars
	chocolate biscuit
Lunch	cheese, ham or tuna salad sandwich on two slices of white bread with butter and mayonnaise
	yoghurt and orange squash
Mid-afternoon	tea with milk and two sugars
	piece of cake or a chocolate biscuit
Evening	meat, fish or chicken with mashed potatoes and vegetables or fish and chips or pizza
	ice cream or cheese and biscuits
Supper	tea with milk and two sugars
	two chocolate biscuits
Alcohol	about 14 units a week

• *Other factors that affect your fitness* •

Smoking and taking drugs will lower your fitness and put your long-term health at risk.

Drugs also contain chemicals that affect the normal functioning of your body. Too much stress may affect your immune system and make you more susceptible to illness.

Your fitness levels can sometime decline as you get older, but that doesn't mean that you are ever too old to start a fitness programme. Being ill will affect how well your body works and therefore how fit you

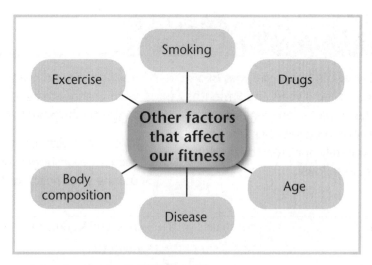

▲ Other factors that affect fitness

are. Different **diseases** are characterised by different signs and symptoms. They are linked to **heredity**, infection, environmental factors or dietary factors. Staying fit will help reduce your risk of disease.

Your body composition can affect how fit you are. Too much body fat may have a negative impact on your health and fitness. Exercise has the biggest effect on your fitness, whatever your age. Regular exercise offers many health benefits:

bones get stronger

improves cardiorespiratory fitness

reduces risk of disease

improves posture

improves body shape and burns body fat

relieves stress

maintains flexibility and suppleness

▲ The benefits of exercise for fitness

EVIDENCE ACTIVITY

Health-related issues

1 Make a list of how sport and leisure activities could help with different health issues. P2

2 Use the information you gathered from your local health practitioner and the Internet to write a short report on how sport and leisure activities could help with different health issues. In this report you need to mention what local and national initiatives there are to improve the nation's health. M2

3 Using the information from the report you wrote for 2, explain how local and national initiatives could influence and are influenced by different health issues. D1

Lifestyle programmes

The term 'lifestyle' refers to your way of life or style of living. There is a large amount of evidence to show that adopting a healthy lifestyle will reduce your risk of disease. Healthy living refers to things like diet, weight, physical activity and stress management. Lifestyle programmes are all about reducing health risks by helping people to live healthier lives.

Lifestyle

Your lifestyle, or the way you live your life, will affect your health and fitness. Do you do any exercise, are you **sedentary** or are you very active? Adopting a healthy lifestyle means you try to balance healthy eating, exercise and your **lifestyle habits**. A healthy lifestyle promotes good health and reduces your risk of disease.

• *Employment and technology* •

Changes to our employment patterns and technology have contributed to us leading more sedentary lifestyles. Many people now work in offices where they spend most of the day sitting at a desk. This means that we need to make time to be physically active each day.

> **GLOSSARY**
>
> **Sedentary** means you do not do any exercise.
> **Lifestyle habits** are all the things that make up the way you live your life e.g. sleep, smoking or having fun.

GIVE IT A GO: lifestyle issues

Visit your local health promotion unit and ask for any leaflets on lifestyle issues such as smoking, physical activity, diet, drug and alcohol use. You may find these leaflets useful in assisting with the lifestyle programmes you need to create for the assessment of this unit.

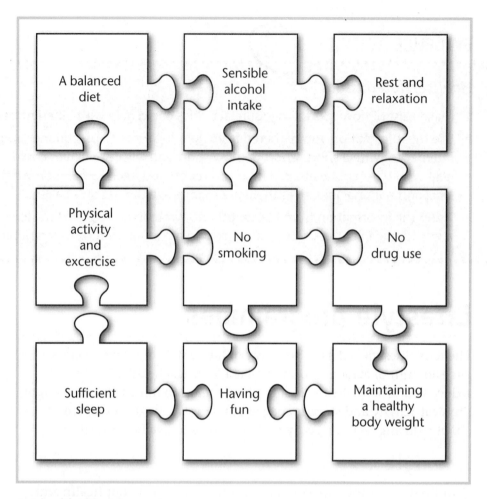

▲ **A healthy lifestyle**

Barriers to adopting a healthy lifestyle

There may be many barriers to adopting a healthy lifestyle. Barriers are factors that stop you from being able get fit and healthy. For example, there may not be any sport or leisure facilities near you, or your religion might prevent you from exercising with people of the opposite sex.

GIVE IT A GO: barriers to adopting a healthy lifestyle

With a partner, write a list of all the reasons you can think of that could stop you from exercising.

Did your list include any of the following?

▷ *money and finances*
▷ *time*

- *location and environment*
- *transport*
- *responsibilities including family and work commitments*
- *attitude and motivation*
- *religious beliefs and practices*
- *peer pressure*
- *illness and disease*
- *education.*

Healthy lifestyle action planning

It is not easy changing your lifestyle. The first step is to think about what you want to change about your lifestyle and then decide how you will go about making the changes.

• *Action planning* •

Putting together an action plan will help you pinpoint what parts of your lifestyle you want to change. When you are putting together a lifestyle programme you must think about the following:

- *what your desired outcomes or goals are – you might want to lose weight or win a race*
- *lifestyle factors – money, time, location etc.*
- *your exercise history – sport you used to play*
- *activity likes and dislikes*
- *any contraindications – disease or illness*
- *time and motivation.*

• *Diet and exercise plans* •

Diet and exercise plans are plans that set out your long- and your short-term objectives or goals for changes to these parts of your lifestyle. For example, your short-term objective might be to run a five-kilometre race by the end of the year, and your long-term goal might be to run a marathon. Diet plans should follow healthy eating and balance of good health principles. Exercise plans should promote the development of all components of health- or skill-related fitness. Your plans should be written down so that you can remind yourself of your goals and so that you can record your progress.

• *Setting goals and objectives* •

The most effective way of setting goals is by setting yourself SMART goals. You are much more likely to be successful! SMART goal setting means being:

Specific – write down exactly what changes you want to make or what goal you are trying to achieve

Measurable – make sure you can measure any changes, for example by doing a fitness test

Agreed and recorded – write down your goals and record your progress

Realistic – set achievable goals

Time framed – set a time when you want to achieve your goals by, to keep you on track.

Healthy lifestyle initiatives

There are many local and national initiatives, such as *Walking your way to health* and *5-a-day*, aimed at improving the nation's health.

GIVE IT A GO: initiatives

1 Using the Internet (links to some helpful websites are available at www.heinemann.co.uk/hotlinks, express code 0005P) or your local health promotion office find out about the range of local and national initiatives aimed at improving the nation's health. Awareness of these initiatives will help you meet the requirements for the assessment of this unit.

 WHAT **if?**

...you were asked to devise a healthy lifestyle initiative?
What kind of initiative would you choose and how would you promote it?

Influences on lifestyle programmes

There are a number of factors that might help or hinder the adoption of healthy lifestyle programmes such as the media, your peers and sporting events like the Olympic Games. Lifestyle issues now feature almost daily in our newspapers, magazines, TV programmes and advertising, while the Internet has become another avenue to promote healthy living.

When considering adopting a healthier lifestyle, the support offered by peers may be invaluable in providing motivation and support. Major sporting events like the Olympics or the World Cup provide a focus for promoting physically active lifestyles and lead to more people becoming interested in the sports involved.

GIVE IT A GO: Lifestyle Assessment Questionnaire

Lifestyle Assessment Questionnaire

The purpose of this questionnaire is to raise your awareness of healthy and unhealthy lifestyle choices you make.

Please answer true or false to the following questions:

1 Diet
I usually try to eat three balanced meals each day
True/False
I usually eat at least 5 servings of fruit/vegetables each day
True/False
I eat the right amount to have a healthy body weight
True/False
I only consume alcohol within the recommended guidelines
True/False

2 Physical Activity and Exercise
I undertake at least 30 minutes of moderate intensity physical activity at least five times per week
True/False

3 Stress
I get plenty of rest
True/False
I seldom feel tense or anxious
True/False

4 Sleep
I usually get at least eight hours of sleep each night
True/False

5 Smoking
I never smoke
True/False

6 Drugs
I never take drugs
True/False

Allow yourself one point for each true answer.
9–10 = very healthy lifestyle
7–8 = generally healthy lifestyle
5–6 = average lifestyle
below 5 = unhealthy lifestyle; many improvements needed

Answering the questionnaire will help you highlight which aspects of your lifestyle require changes to improve your health. If you have many aspects to change, prioritise these and start with the changes you know you can easily make first.

CASE STUDY – PUTTING IT ALL TOGETHER

John is a 30-year-old business man. He is married with two young children, aged six and four. Recently he has become increasingly concerned about his expanding waistline. He's always tired and has also noticed that he is having difficulty keeping up with his children on their weekend outing to the local park.

John works long hours, leaving the house at 6.30am. For breakfast he grabs a pastry and coffee at the train station on the way to work. For lunch, John either attends a business lunch at the local Italian restaurant or he skips it altogether.

Due to the demands of his job John often gets home late after his wife and children have eaten. He then eats his meal in front of the television with a glass of red wine and he sometimes drinks half a bottle a night to help him relax.

His long working hours give him little time to enjoy his membership of the local health club and he is thinking of giving up his membership, as he feels he is not getting value for money. He also used to enjoy playing football for the local Sunday league team.

1 How would you summarise John's lifestyle?

2 What potential barriers do you think there are to John adopting a healthier lifestyle?

3 What changes would you recommend to John's lifestyle?

4 Devise a diet programme for John taking into account healthy eating and National Food Guide principles.

5 Devise an exercise programme for John taking into account current recommendations for physical activity.

EVIDENCE ACTIVITY

Lifestyle programmes

As you have discovered, lifestyle programmes are a way to improve an individual's health and reduce their risk of disease.

1 Identify two different individuals and produce lifestyle programmes to meet their needs.

2 Explain how the plans you have devised in **1**, should improve the individuals' health and reduce their risk of disease.

Find the answers to the questions in the puzzle. They could be written across, down or diagonally, backwards or forwards.

H	A	J	O	X	Y	G	E	N	B	X	T	S	G
Z	E	D	E	C	N	A	L	A	B	K	R	H	F
V	E	P	L	F	D	S	Y	N	C	V	A	C	U
L	O	U	N	D	Y	H	E	A	M	L	M	E	R
A	T	L	M	U	T	E	N	D	O	N	S	O	N
T	E	S	U	N	O	A	E	L	T	H	I	M	N
E	E	E	I	L	T	L	M	P	Q	B	Z	V	U
L	P	O	C	F	I	T	N	E	S	S	S	T	T
E	B	O	L	F	J	H	E	P	U	N	I	L	R
K	J	L	A	R	H	S	F	E	U	Y	L	N	I
S	K	L	C	O	U	Y	R	F	G	K	V	N	E
S	E	T	A	R	D	Y	H	O	B	R	A	C	N
Z	N	R	K	L	D	H	K	M	S	P	O	T	T
M	O	E	N	M	O	P	O	R	D	H	A	K	S

1 The state of complete physical, psychological and social well being can be defined as _____?

2 The ability to meet the demands of your environment can be defined as _____?

3 Which body system helps you maintain your posture and provides attachment for your muscles?

4 What attaches your muscles to your bones?

5 What is transported by your blood from your lungs into your body?

6 Your body's main sources of energy are known as _____?

7 You require this mineral for growth and repair of your bones.

8 A balanced diet will supply all the _____ your needs body.

9 To encourage success when lifestyle programming, your goals should be_____?

10 Healthy eating means having a _____ diet?

unit 4

Personal effectiveness

Personal effectiveness is about making the most of your personal resources in relation to what is important to you. This includes your talents, knowledge, skills and motivation. In this unit you will explore your own potential by doing an audit of your personal and work-related skills. You will learn how to look for jobs in the sport and leisure industry that interest you and that are suited to your talents and skills. At the end of the unit you will write your own curriculum vitae and start to build a personal portfolio to present to potential employers.

You will have the opportunity to improve your own learning and performance by agreeing targets, attempting to meet them and reviewing your progress. You will use information technology to find information that will support you in developing your personal effectiveness, as well as to present information to potential employers. A key aim of this unit is to match your individual strengths to specific job roles and your employment ambitions.

The activities in this unit will help you to get to know yourself better and understand what you want from a job or career. They will also help you recognise what others will expect of you in certain job roles.

This unit is internally assessed. This means, to pass this unit, you will complete an assignment set and marked by your tutor.

In this unit you will need to learn about:

- ▭ carrying out a personal audit to help you find a suitable job
- ▭ exploring your potential in relation to suitable jobs
- ▭ preparing a personal statement and portfolio to prepare for employment.

Personal audit

A **personal audit** is a review of your skills and experiences so far. This **self-assessment** can help you plan where you want to go with your job and career. It is about figuring out where you are now, where you want to go and planning how you will get there.

Looking for a job

Looking for a job in the sport and leisure industry is not just about qualifications. Having a range of personal and work-related skills is also important. Different careers and jobs will require different qualifications and skills. Fortunately, in the UK the sport and leisure industry is booming and there is a vast range of paid and unpaid jobs available to you. Before you do your own personal audit you will find it useful to have an idea of the skills and qualifications needed for the various jobs that interest you.

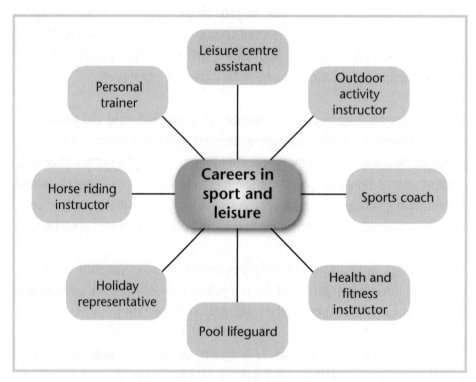

▲ Some of the jobs on offer in the sport and leisure industry

Doing a personal audit

A personal audit involves looking at what vocational, personal, interpersonal and behavioural skills you have. It also includes looking at your interests and hobbies.

▲ A fitness instructor needs good interpersonal skills

EVIDENCE ACTIVITY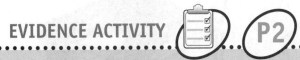

Researching possible jobs

1 Log onto the Connections website – the new youth service for providing advice and guidance on personal development and career planning (a link to this website is available at www.heinemann.co.uk/hotlinks, express code 0005P).

2 Make a list of a range of jobs or careers in sport and leisure that interest you. For example, you might want to look at the role of a leisure centre assistant, outdoor activity instructor, sports coach or health and fitness instructor.

If you do not have access to the Internet check out some of the industry magazines, such as *Leisure Management* and *Leisure Opportunities*, or have a look in your local newspaper. Pay particular attention to the qualifications and skills required by the jobs and careers that interest you.

● *Vocational skills* ●

Your vocational skills are your work-related experiences, for example any part-time jobs, work experience or voluntary work you might have done. Don't forget to include any vocational qualifications you may have, such as a First Aid certificate, life saving award or community sports leader awards. For many jobs and careers in the sport and leisure industry vocational qualifications are recognised and in studying for this qualification you are already preparing yourself for a career in sport or leisure.

● *Personal and interpersonal skills* ●

Your personal skills are skills that relate to your appearance, body language and posture. Interpersonal skills are related to how you get on with people and, in particular, how you might get on with colleagues in the work place.For example, you may work very well in a team – this is an interpersonal skill – or you may have open body language – this is a personal skill.

▲ Our body posture sends out messages about our confidence and attitude

● *Behaviour* ●

Behaviour is the way you act around other people. Professional behaviour at work helps to maintain high standards and set a professional image. Expected behaviour in the workplace is often governed by codes of conduct or practice. It is very important to understand what behaviour is expected in the work place. For example, arriving on time, not drinking alcohol at work and being helpful and friendly to team members are all expected ways of behaving. Sometimes this might mean changing your behaviour, for example, making an effort not to hum your favourite song in an open-plan office.

● *Interests* ●

Hobbies such as music, film, theatre, sport and outdoor activities say something about what your interests are. Looking at your interests can be the starting point for choosing a career in sport and leisure – if you love to horse-ride, you could look for a job at a stable or as a Lipizzaner trainer.

You can develop your interests into work-related skills. For example, you may have a particular talent for something, such as organising people or competence in a particular sport. You could then look for a job that makes use of these talents, such as managing a sport team or organising leisure events for your local council.

GIVE IT A GO: what skills do I have?

1 Make a list of all the vocational skills and qualifications you have gained to date.
2 Make a note of any personal and interpersonal skills that might help you to be successful in a job.
3 Make a list of your hobbies, interests and talents.
All this information will be essential when you start to write your curriculum vitae.

EVIDENCE ACTIVITY   P1

1 Draw up a list summarising your main job-related skills and qualifications. You can use the information you gathered in the *Give it a go* activity above.

2 Use information technology to present this in a logical and structured format.

Potential

Your potential refers to any abilities or talents that you have not yet developed. You may have abilities and talents that can contribute to your personal effectiveness at work that you have not yet discovered or worked on.

Strengths

Your strengths are all the positive characteristics you have that you can bring into a job. They are skills that are under your control – that means you can change them or learn new strengths. You need to think about what strengths you can bring to any job that interests you. Strengths can be work experience, education or training, strong technical knowledge, specific **transferable skills**, personal characteristics, useful contacts or links to professional organisations.

▲ **Do you have any of these strengths?**

Weaknesses

Your weaknesses are negative characteristics that are also under your control. These might be lack of relevant work experience, education or training, poor technical knowledge, lack of transferable skills and poor personal and interpersonal skills. You can plan to improve upon your weaknesses.

GIVE IT A GO: improving your weaknesses

1 Create a table like the one below and list two of your weaknesses.

2 What can you do to turn these weaknesses into strengths?

Weakness	What can I do to improve?

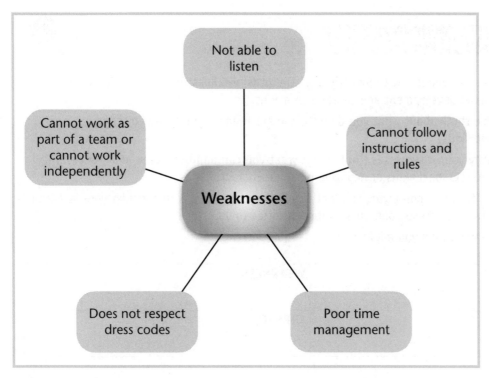

▲ **Do you have any of these weaknesses?**

Self-assessment

During a self-assessment you will look in detail at what your strengths and weaknesses are. You will then match your strengths to potential job roles or careers and set your self an action plan to evaluate, monitor and review your progress.

• *A SWOT analysis* •

A **SWOT** analysis is a useful way of identifying your strengths and weaknesses. It can also be used to identify the opportunities and **threats** you face and is a useful first step in finding career. A SWOT analysis will help you to maximise your strengths, minimise your weaknesses and take advantage of the opportunities available to you, whilst being aware of the potential threats to your success.

GLOSSARY

SWOT stands for strengths, weakness, opportunities and threats.
Threats are the obstacles you might face.

GIVE IT A GO: SWOT analysis

Use a SWOT table like the one below to identify any strengths, weaknesses, opportunities and threats to your personal development and career aspirations.

- For your strengths, think about what you do well, the experiences you have, your personal characteristics and skills.
- To help you identify your weaknesses think about what you can improve, weak areas of technical knowledge and interpersonal skills or negative personal characteristics.
- A useful approach to take when trying to identify your opportunities is to consider your strengths and ask yourself whether these open up any opportunities to you.
- Your threats are any barriers you might face.

STRENGTHS	WEAKNESSES
OPPORTUNITIES	THREATS

CASE STUDY – PETER

Peter wants to be a fitness instructor. Fitness instructors require a specialist qualification in instructing group exercise or giving one-to-one instruction. They should have good communication and interpersonal skills, and a reasonable level of personal fitness. They need to be able to motivate people and work on their own initiative.

Peter's personal information:

Name: Peter Delalio

Current position: Working as a part-time bar assistant

Career aims: To become a fitness instructor or manager

Previous achievements, experience, skills and interests:

- NVQ level 1 Assistant Fitness Instructor Award
- pool lifeguard award
- six weeks' work experience at the local leisure centre, working on a children's activity camp
- uses the gym regularly to improve and maintain personal fitness levels.

Personal skills:

- able to work on own initiative
- highly motivated
- smart and punctual.

Peter read the following advert in the local newspaper, advertising for an assistant leisure co-ordinator.

a Which of Peter's job-related strengths will help him to succeed in this job?

b Make a list of any of Peter's weaknesses that will make it difficult for him to succeed in this job?

c What should Peter's next step be?

Assistant Leisure Co-ordinator

Shapeup Leisure Centre

We are looking for an assistant leisure co-ordinator to work closely with our senior leisure co-ordinator in the day-to-day operation of our leisure facility which includes the swimming pool and fitness suites.

It is essential that you have good communication skills, a strong commitment to creating one of the best leisure facilities in the area and the ability to work on your own initiative as well as part of a team. Flexibility is essential as shift working, including weekends and bank holidays, is an integral part of the job.

Ideally you should have a fitness instructor qualification and previous industry experience.

EVIDENCE ACTIVITY   P3

From the personal audit that you completed on page 85, work out what your job-related strengths and weaknesses are.

Action planning

Knowing yourself is the starting point to planning a career path that is right for you. In addition to your skills and abilities, it is important to understand what interests you, your personality and your motivations.

The next step is to use the knowledge you have gained about yourself to write an action plan.

An action plan will help you to:

- *focus your attention*
- *take steps to plan for your future job or career*
- *gain further skills that might be important to your chosen career*
- *recognise and keep a record of your achievements to date*
- *apply for jobs and relevant work experience*
- *improve your confidence at being successful.*

Action planning involves setting yourself **targets** and deciding how you are going to achieve them. Now that you have spent time doing your personal audit of your skills and have found some job roles that you are interested in, you need to set some goals and objectives. Remember to make sure that your objectives are SMART (to recap setting SMART goals read pages 75–76 in Unit 3).

GIVE IT A GO: writing an action plan

Use the personal goal setting and action planner below to set yourself SMART goals.

To help you the headings are explained:

- objective – what you want to try to achieve
- action – the steps you will take to try and achieve your goal
- time – when you want to have achieved your goal by
- measure – how you will know you have achieved your goal
- resources – the resources or support you need to help you achieve your goal
- barriers – things that might get in the way of you being successful.

Personal goal setting and action planner				
Objective	**Action**	**Time**	**Measure**	**Resources Barriers**
1				
2				
3				
4				
5				
6				

EVIDENCE ACTIVITY  P4

Develop an action plan to improve your strengths and weaknesses over a period of time. Use the information you have gathered in the previous *Give it a go* activity, to help you write your plan.

Personal statement and portfolio

Somewhere out there in the job market there is at least one employer, if not several, who will be interested in employing you. However, you have to convince them that you have the necessary skills and personal qualities to do the job. To do this you need to be positive about yourself and be sure that the job you apply for is the one that you want.

Curriculum vitae

Your **curriculum vitae** (CV) is a short summary of your educational and employment background, which you give to potential employers when you are applying for a job. It is a very important document and is your key marketing tool – it has to show the best of you. A well produced CV will tell potential employers important information such as your qualifications and experience as well as your personal and job-related skills.

CVs usually contain four key sections of information:

- ▭ *personal details*
- ▭ *education*
- ▭ *employment history*
- ▭ *information relevant to the job.*

Your personal details will include your name, address and contact details. The education section will highlight the qualifications you have obtained and when. Employment history will detail who you have worked for, including any volunteer work you have done. You should start the employment sections with your most recent employer first.

> ### GLOSSARY
>
> **Curriculum vitae** literally translated means the course of one's life.

WHAT if?

...I don't have a CV?

Write a list of all the reasons why you should write a CV and keep it up to date.
You might want to think about this from a potential employer's point of view as well as your own.

GIVE IT A GO: rejecting CVs

1 Spend a few minutes thinking about why CVs are rejected by potential employers.
2 Now have a look at the diagram below to compare your ideas. Discuss your answers with a partner.

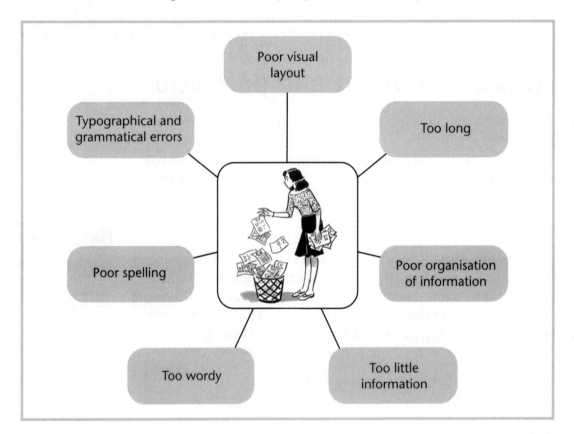

GLOSSARY

Recruits are new employees.
Shortlisting means to make a shortlist with the names of the best people.

From an employer's point of view, a CV saves time and money as they don't need to give out application forms to **recruits**. It is also an essential part of **shortlisting** potential recruits for interview. If you produce a good CV that is well structured and informative it shows that you can manage information and communicate well. From your point of view it helps you to promote yourself to potential employers. You must update your CV regularly as you gain new skills and work experience.

● *Writing your CV* ●

As you start on this process keep in mind that there is no one 'correct' way to write your CV. Your CV is a unique summary of your personal experiences which will be different from those of others. It is also important to always adjust your CV to suit the job you are applying for. When reading CVs, employers will look for relevant skills, qualifications and achievements and what you can do for them in a particular job, so sending out one standard CV is not the best way to market yourself.

● *CV checklist* ●

Before sending your CV to potential employers make sure you have:

▷ *looked at the job avert and job description carefully*
▷ *researched the company or organisation you are hoping to work for*
▷ *adjusted your CV to the job advertised and what the employer will be looking for*
▷ *been clear about what qualifications, skills, experience and qualities are essential for the job role and shown evidence that you have these*
▷ *made your CV interesting and easy to read*
▷ *asked for advice and feedback from your careers advisor, personal tutor or other appropriate person.*

● *Job descriptions* ●

When applying for a job it is important to start by reading the advertisement or job description very carefully. It may not be obvious what skills and qualities the employer is looking for. It is also a good idea to do some research on the company. Look at the advertisement in the case study on page 94. Although it is not written in the advertisement, Suntripper Holidays will be looking for the following skills and qualities in a lifeguard:

▷ *good interpersonal skills*
▷ *an ability to work in a team*
▷ *the ability to take initiative*
▷ *someone with a smart appearance*
▷ *fun-loving personality*
▷ *responsible because of the safety aspects involved in the job*
▷ *lifeguarding qualification.*

GIVE IT A GO: writing your CV

1 Look in your local newspaper, magazines or on the Connections website (a link to this website is available at www.heinemann.co.uk/hotlinks, express code 0005P) for a job that you might like to apply for. After reading the job advertisement carefully, try writing a CV to support an application for the job. Use the checklist above to help you.

● *The covering letter* ●

You have now written your CV and received some feedback on it. However, CVs cannot be sent to potential employers alone, you will also need a covering letter to go with it.

CASE STUDY – COMPARING CVS

Have a look at the two CVs written in response to the Suntripper Holiday, Lifeguard advertisement shown below.

Suntripper Holidays

Lifeguards Required

Looking for excitement and a life changing experience?
Want the opportunity to be paid for working in the sun?

We have exclusive beach resorts all over the Med including Greece, Turkey and Italy dedicated to holidaymakers who worship the sun, sea and surf. Your job would be to ensure our holiday makers feel safe and reassured as they enjoy our friendly holiday environment. We offer a great package including full board and use of our water sports and activity facilities.

If you are over 18, have a life guarding qualification, a great personality and want a summer to remember, send your CV to Pat Jones, Suntripper Resorts Recruitment, Sunshine House, Charles Street, Birmingham, B4 3JT

▲ **Advertisement**

Alison Smith
3 Prince Street
Birmingham
B1 9PS

Tel: 0121 3456789
Email: a.smith@abc.com

Education/Qualifications:
• BTEC Certificate in Sport and Leisure
• National Pool Lifeguard Award
• Assistant Fitness Instructor Award

Employment History:
During the summer holidays I have worked as a pool lifeguard at my local leisure centre. I also work part-time at weekends as a waitress in a cafe.

Interests:
I enjoy water sports, aerobics, going out socially with my friends and holidaying with my family.

Additional Information:
I have an outgoing personality and friendly nature and would welcome the opportunity for foreign travel to experience different countries and cultures.

References:
Can be supplied on request.

▲ **Alison Smith's CV**

Ajay Ikbar
5 Charles Street
Birmingham
B8 10DP

Tel: 0121 9876 543

Education/Qualifications:
2004: BTEC Certificate in Sport and Leisure
2003: National Pool Lifeguard Award
2002: Community Sports Leader Award

Employment History:
I work part time as a pool lifeguard at my local leisure centre.
During the summer holidays I also worked as an assistant
activities co-ordinator on an activity camp for children.

Interests:
I enjoy all aspects of fitness and play football for my local team
for which I am vice captain. I enjoy foreign travel and recently
spent 3 weeks back-packing round the Med with a group of
friends.

Additional Information:
Acting as vice captain of my football team has enabled me to
develop leadership, communication and teamwork skills
essential to this position. In addition, working at the children's
activity camp often required me to act on my own initiative
when organising activities to ensure all chidren had an
enjoyable camp experience.

References:
Can be supplied on request.

▲ Ajay Ikbar's CV

1 What skills and qualities are Suntripper Holidays looking for?

2 Copy the table below and make a list of Alison Smith's strengths and weaknesses in relation to the job role advertised.

3 Again, using the table, make a list of Ajay Ikbar's strengths and weaknesses in relation to the job role advertised.

4 Who is the most suitable applicant for the job? Why?

Alison Smith		Ajay Ikbar	
Strengths	Weaknesses	Strengths	Weaknesses

...I don't write a covering letter?

With a partner discuss why you think a covering letter is important. Be ready to share your ideas with the rest of the class.

Employers may get several, if not hundreds, of applications for a job. Your covering letter helps you to introduce yourself and personalise your application. You can use it to make the reasons why you are applying for the job clear and show that you have a good understanding of what the job will involve. It gives you the chance to summarise your transferable skills and most importantly it should encourage your potential employer to read your CV. In your covering letter you should highlight the key skills, attributes and work experience that are needed in the job. A poor covering letter may mean your CV is rejected without even being read.

Remember, as with your CV, it is good practice to get feedback from your careers advisor, personal tutor or other appropriate person before sending it off with your CV.

GIVE IT A GO: writing a covering letter

Write a covering letter to support the CV you wrote in the *Give it a go* activity on page 93.

● *Application forms* ●

Some employers prefer application forms because it means they can compare all applicants' answers to the same questions. Again there are some simple rules for completing application forms successfully.

Make sure that you:

- *read the form carefully first before putting pen to paper*
- *photocopy the form several times to give yourself the opportunity to practise*
- *fill in the form as requested, following the instructions and using black ink*
- *give enough detail and evidence to back up any statements you make about yourself or the job role*
- *get someone else to check it for spelling, grammatical errors and to give you some feedback*
- *photocopy the form before you send it off to keep a record for interview purposes*
- *send it off with a covering letter in a suitably sized envelope.*

Application forms are also used by colleges and training organisations. If you are not looking to enter the world of work yet, you might be looking at options for further study. Application forms for courses or further study often ask you to produce a **personal statement** or application essay.

● *Your personal statement* ●

Your personal statement is your chance to sell yourself. You can write about personal qualities that are not developed elsewhere in the application form. It is **self-reflective** and lets you focus on your achievements and goals. As with CVs there is no single correct way to write a personal statement.

Getting started on writing your personal statement is probably the hardest part. Time and patience are needed. You might find it frustrating and self-reflection difficult, but it can be a very rewarding task. At the end of the process you should have a personal statement you are proud of.

GLOSSARY

A **personal statement** is a written statement about yourself. It gives you the chance to show your personal attributes.

GLOSSARY

Self-reflection is a personal examination of your experiences.

▲ Writing a personal statement can be frustrating and difficult

 WHAT if?

...*I am asked to write a personal statement?*
When applying for courses why do you think you might be asked to provide a personal statement?

There are some simple rules for writing good personal statements:

- *use the computer to word process it*
- *write why you want to do a particular course or subject*
- *include information on your career ambitions*
- *write about your hobbies and interests and what you gain from them*
- *mention your personal characteristics and transferable skills and what they would bring to the job*
- *show that you are confident about your abilities and experiences*
- *use a good structure, logical presentation and flow*
- *attempt lots of drafts before producing your final version*
- *get someone else to check it for spelling, grammatical errors and to give you feedback on what you have written*
- *keep a copy on file in your personal portfolio.*

EVIDENCE ACTIVITY   P5

Using the information you have collected during your personal audit, pages 82–85, write a personal statement suitable to send to potential employers or with an application to study further.

Portfolios

Portfolios are made up of samples of your work that can provide evidence of your talents, skills and personal characteristics. Traditionally portfolios have been presented in folders or binders, but information technology means they can be presented in disk format too. They can be time consuming to put together, but are useful to take to an interview.

▲ What is in my portfolio?

● *Putting your personal portfolio together* ●

There are some simple rules for compiling a portfolio:

▭ *see which skills are essential for the job you are looking for*
▭ *add evidence that shows you have the relevant skills e.g. certificates*
▭ *give evidence of your previous work experience e.g. an appraisal form*
▭ *present your evidence in a logical and effective format*
▭ *seek feedback on your portfolio from your careers advisor, personal tutor or other appropriate person*
▭ *keep it up to date.*

GIVE IT A GO: your personal portfolio

Copy out the table below.

1 Make a list of the items that you already have for your personal portfolio.
2 Make a list of items you could collect to develop your personal portfolio further.

Items I already have	Items that I can develop

● *Interviews* ●

Your application has been successful and you have been invited to an interview. Interviews can be nerve-wracking experiences, but they are an important part of the process. Remember you are also interviewing the company to see if you would like to work for them. You should also use the interview as a chance to promote yourself to your best advantage. Doing this requires careful preparation.

Preparing for interviews

There are some useful steps that you can take to prepare yourself well for interview. Make sure that you have:

▭ *understood the nature of the job or position for which you are applying*
▭ *researched the company or organisation you are hoping to work for – a starting point could be their website*
▭ *prepared some answers to commonly asked or predictable questions*
▭ *planned what you are going to wear*
▭ *arrived in plenty of time and know where you are going*
▭ *been polite to all staff during the interview experience.*

GIVE IT A GO: an interview

1 Look back to your job application for the *Give it a go* activity on page 93.

2 Make a list of some of the questions you think would be asked at an interview.

The following might be some of the questions to expect.

- Why did you choose sport and leisure as a course of study?
- What is it about this job that interests you?
- What are your strengths and weaknesses in relation to the job role?
- What do you know about our organisation or company?
- Tell us about any relevant work experience you have that is directly related to this job?

3 Role play an interview with your partner, asking the questions you have prepared. Each have a go being the applicant or the interviewer.

The interview

▲ **Remember to look at the person asking the question**

At the interview it is essential not to panic and keep calm. Being well prepared should help you. Remember it is vital to make a good impression. This is very important right from the start of the interview. Don't forget to smile and try to make eye contact with all the interviewers, if there is more than one. Your body language is important too, so watch your posture. Good posture displays confidence. Watch your nervous mannerisms like flicking your hair or fiddling with your glasses.

At interview always:

- *look at the person asking the question*
- *listen carefully to the question*
- *ask the interviewer to repeat the question if you haven't understood it*
- *answer the question clearly and concisely providing an example to reinforce your answer where possible*
- *be enthusiastic.*

Do not:

- *turn up looking scruffy and disinterested*
- *show off and come across as a 'know it all'*
- *mumble*
- *give one-word answers.*

WHAT if?

...they ask me difficult questions?

Think about how you would answer the following tricky questions.

1 What would you like to be doing in five years time?

2 Why should our company employ you?

3 What is your proudest achievement to date?

4 Would you like to ask us any questions?

After the interview

You should review your own performance directly after an interview. Think about what the interview was like and about any questions you found particularly difficult to answer. You should also think about any parts of your interview performance that you might want to improve. Set yourself an action plan to help you with this. If you are unsuccessful, try to think of the interview as a learning experience. You can use the experience to spur you on to do better next time. You can also try to seek feedback from the interviewer about your performance.

Letter of acceptance

You have just found out you have been offered the job. A well-written letter of acceptance can help you get off to a good start with your new employer. The letter's purpose is to accept the job, confirm the terms of your employment and to positively reinforce the employer's confidence in choosing to offer you the position.

When writing acceptance letters make sure that you:

- *word process it*
- *open by thanking whoever sent you the job offer*
- *make it clear you have decided to accept the job*
- *express how much you are looking forward to starting the job*
- *attempt drafts before producing your final version*
- *get someone else to check it for spelling, grammar and to give you feedback*
- *keep a copy on file.*

WORD SEARCH

Find the answers to the questions in the puzzle. They could be written across, down or diagonally, backwards or forwards.

I	T	N	E	M	E	S	I	T	R	E	V	D	A
N	I	C	O	Z	J	P	M	K	X	L	T	E	P
T	I	O	O	N	U	P	V	S	M	A	R	T	O
E	R	V	Q	N	U	Y	B	M	A	N	R	W	I
R	H	E	B	M	N	P	V	X	C	O	M	Y	L
P	V	R	X	L	T	E	O	R	N	I	L	P	O
E	Y	I	E	P	N	R	C	O	L	T	R	G	F
R	Z	N	V	B	W	S	M	T	T	A	Y	U	T
S	P	G	K	X	Q	O	K	J	I	C	E	I	R
O	O	G	S	N	J	N	W	I	E	O	I	Y	O
N	O	D	S	I	F	A	F	N	H	V	N	L	P
A	D	U	R	C	B	L	M	C	O	F	G	S	D
L	K	L	D	I	N	T	E	R	V	I	E	W	A
V	E	L	B	A	R	E	F	S	N	A	R	T	R

1 The new youth service available on the Internet for providing advice and guidance on personal development and career planning is called_____.

2 Your work-related experience is referred to as your _____ skills.

3 Which kind of skills send out messages about how you get on with people?

4 What kind of skills show your ability to transfer your knowledge and skills from one situation to another?

5 When action planning what kind of goals should you aim to set yourself?

6 What kind of letter should always go with your CV?

7 When applying for a particular job it is important to start by reading this carefully.

8 This kind of statement gives you the chance to sell yourself.

9 This is a collection that gives evidence of your talents, skills and personal characteristics.

10 If your CV is good enough you might be lucky enough to be invited to one of these.

unit 5

Social responsibility at work

In this unit you will look at what you, as an employee, can contribute to your working environment. This includes learning about the environment you work in, the laws that govern workplaces, employment issues and working healthily and safely. Ideally this unit's work should be based on a real workplace (maybe during your placement) so that you can see how an organisation and its staff tackle some of the issues, such as pollution, recycling and safety.

Although the topics in this unit may sound a bit daunting you will find that they talk about everyday parts of work, which you probably know something about already. This unit looks at how you can learn from and contribute to good practice in your working environment.

This unit is internally assessed. This means that, to pass this unit, you will complete an assignment set and marked by your tutor.

In this unit you will need to learn about:

- environmental issues at work
- how the law affects people at work.

Environmental issues

Many people are becoming much more aware of the need to have **sustainable approaches** to using resources. This means looking for ways to save on waste and the use of energy. People are thinking how they can help keep the environment free from pollution and poisonous gases, which cause **global warming** and other problems. If everyone makes a small effort a difference can be made to our climate in the future.

▲ Everyone can learn to recycle waste

Over the last few years many countries have signed up to environmental treaties to help slow down the effects of global warming and set targets for waste disposal (**Agenda 21** and **Kyoto agreements**). What we do at home and at work can also make a difference.

Organisations, such as Youth Act (a link to their website is available at www.heinemann.co.uk/hotlinks express code 0005P), are trying to clean up parks and play areas. This is about campaigning for and achieving change in your community. Two groups of young people from Seven Sisters, in London, are doing just that. They want to get their filthy parks cleaned up. The climbing frames have been replaced and the litter, like condoms and syringes, has been removed to make it a safe play area for children.

GIVE IT A GO: What can I do to help?

1 Working with a partner, design a form which you could use to carry out a survey around your college or school. Use the form to note any:

   a efforts to recycle

   b rubbish bins

   c efforts to save energy.

3 Evaluate whether you think these are enough and if they are being well used.

4 Make some recommendations on how your college or school could improve its environmental responsibility.

Environmental issues at work

Many sport and leisure organisations are also looking at ways to be more environmentally friendly. The following diagram shows some of the ways companies can make sure that their workplaces are environmentally friendly.

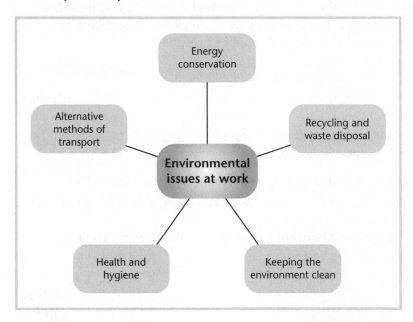

▲ **Environmental issues at work**

Energy conservation

The sport and leisure industry use a lot of energy in the running of sport and leisure centres. They have to heat, ventilate and light large areas of space such as sports halls, swimming pools and outdoor playing areas.

GLOSSARY

Energy conservation means saving energy.

GLOSSARY

Energy efficient means using as little power or resources as possible.

GLOSSARY

Recycling is using materials again by making them into other things.

● *Saving costs* ●

It is important that sport and leisure centre managers buy the cheapest sources of energy, but also the most **energy efficient**. Doing this will also give the facility long-term financial savings.

This might mean focussing on:

- ▭ *using energy-efficient lighting systems*
- ▭ *recycling of warm air*
- ▭ *using timers and sensors to switch off power*
- ▭ *solar-powered heating*
- ▭ *reducing amounts of water used.*

Look out for the 'Energy Efficiency Recommended' logo when you are buying electrical appliances. The logo appears on a growing range of products – from light bulbs to laundry appliances. This logo shows which appliances are the most energy efficient and therefore cheaper to run.

⬭ THINK ABOUT IT

If every old, energy-inefficient fridge-freezer was replaced by a new Energy Efficiency Recommended one it could save each household that made the change £35 every year in electricity bills. If we all made the change this week, together we'd save over £500 million every year!

Can you think of any disadvantages of doing this?

If you cannot buy energy-efficient appliances or products, costs can be cut by action from staff members. This might mean:

- ▭ *regular checks to ensure that lights not being used are switched off*
- ▭ *making sure that machines that are not needed have been turned off e.g. extractor fans or vehicle engines*
- ▭ *ensuring that the activity area temperature is at a constant temperature*
- ▭ *closing doors to keep heat in.*

GIVE IT A GO: energy efficiency

Visit or contact your local leisure centre and ask:

   a if they run any machines that are energy efficient

   b how they ensure staff are aware of energy efficiency.

● *Use of bio-degradable materials* ●

Some examples of the kind of **bio-degradable** materials found in sports and leisure centres are:

▭ *bio-degradable waste sacks for grass and weeds – some plastics are totally degradable. They decompose by heat, light, time, stress and bio-activity. This would be particularly useful for local authorities that have large areas of parkland and pitches to maintain*

▭ *non-chemical-based detergents and cleaners – these could be used by leisure centres with food outlets*

▭ *bio-degradable packaging – leisure venues with take-away and vending facilities could use bio-degradable food and drink containers*

▭ *natural materials – using straw as a temporary barrier at a race track.*

As part of your assessment you need to identify and discuss the environmentally friendly activities which are important in a job role, so try to spot if any similar methods are used at your workplace.

GIVE IT A GO: proof of environmentally friendly practices

1 With a partner design a form, make a poster or take some photographs, which you could use to record evidence of environmentally friendly practices at work. Look for things that fit under the range of headings found in this last section.

2 Present your findings to the rest of the class.

● *Disposal* ●

Disposal methods are a key part of ensuring you are environmentally friendly. European Union regulations have outlined many ways companies can get rid of their waste in an environmentally friendly way. Some of these methods are used in sports and leisure venues such as, the disposal of:

▭ *cleaning fluids and chemicals from swimming pools*
▭ *old racing tyres from race tracks*
▭ *waste products from people and animals after a big dog or cat show.*

Recycling

Some environmentalists say that anything can be used again. Here are some unusual examples:

- *mouse-mats made from circuit boards*
- *coasters from yoghurt pots*
- *toothbrushes and folders from juice cartons.*

Other more common examples are:

- *recycling paper, glass and cans*
- *recycling computers and mobile phones*
- *equipment being repaired or renovated instead of being thrown away.*

All of these types of recycling mean you are not only saving money, but also materials too.

Cleaner environment

In the sports and leisure industry having a cleaner environment means having cleaner air at venues, cleaner land-based play areas and cleaner stretches of water.

• *Air quality* •

The quality of the air, or how clean it is, is an important issue for athletes, people taking active leisure and children. Venues close to busy roads or with big parking areas, such as stadiums or shopping malls, can become unhealthy environments because of the amount of poisonous gas in exhaust fumes.

GLOSSARY

Eco-efficient means to use the smallest amount of natural products and to keep waste to a minimum. **Flame retardants** are sprayed onto materials to slow down burning. They are often poisonous.

CASE STUDY – ECO-FRIENDLY COMPANIES

Many top companies are setting out new eco-friendly objectives as part of their business plans. Some of their ideas might be to:

- only use **eco-efficient** products and services
- use lead-free electronics and manufacturing processes, with an aim of introducing the first 100% lead-free products in 2007
- reduce the poisonous effects of **flame retardants** and other fluids

- reduce the amount of energy needed to make new products.

1 What are the environmental benefits of each of these ideas?

2 Can you find any examples of sports products or organisations that follow these business plans? These types of examples might give you good discussion points for your assessment.

▲ **Exhaust fumes lower the quality of the air**

The countryside does not have the same levels of **air pollution** as cities and built-up areas. People living in the countryside often do not suffer from as many lung-related illnesses, such as asthma and coughs.

Indoor sports and leisure venues should have filter systems installed to help keep the air clean, especially if there are large numbers of sweaty people using the facility every day.

• *Litter and waste* •

Keeping **litter** and **waste** under control is a big issue for leisure organisations such as cinemas and stadiums. For example, after every match at a stadium people leave litter in the stands. Litter is very expensive and difficult to clean up. Some large venues will hire people to come in and clear up after sport and leisure events.

> **GLOSSARY**
>
> **Air pollution** refers to gases that make the air dirty, for example, smoke from factories.

> **GLOSSARY**
>
> **Litter** and **waste** includes everything from plastic bottles or containers to left over food.

▲ **Clearing up a stadium can be a costly business**

● *Public health policies in the workplace* ●

The government makes laws that are meant to help us live in a cleaner environment; these are called **public health policies**. There are a number of laws that affect the workplace, such as anti-smoking and drinking regulations, lighting and radiation.

Anti-smoking regulations

Smoking is banned from most sports and leisure venues. Many more public places are also banning smoking indoors – Ireland has recently banned smoking in all its pubs. You can often see people smoking at the entrance to office buildings which can give a very poor first impression for new visitors.

Anti-alcohol regulations

There are very strict drinking regulations in all areas of sport and leisure. Most coaches going to sports matches have bans on drinking alcohol, as do most football stadiums. Leisure areas often set limits on the amount of alcohol that can be drunk in public places; some even ban drinking on the street. Certainly drinking at work could result in disciplinary action or probably dismissal for an employee.

WHAT if?

... *we did not have drinking regulations?*

Discuss with others in your class why we need to have drinking regulations at sport and leisure venues. Why are these regulations more relaxed at cricket grounds?

Lighting

The right kind of lighting is important in some areas of sport and leisure in order to create professional standards and safe playing environments. Some of these include:

- ▭ *height and angles over playing courts e.g. for badminton*
- ▭ *density and intensity for night play e.g. football and cricket matches*
- ▭ *glare and shadows e.g. in drivers' eyes at evening races*
- ▭ *over car parks or walkways to increase security.*

Radiation

We are becoming more aware of the dangers of **radiation** as research has shown that there can be some harmful effects from the over-use of mobile phones, computers or headphones. Some communities have even begun to protest against putting telephone masts up near schools and leisure centres. Other harmful effects can be found where food is kept warm under heat lamps for a long time or where sunbeds are used.

▲ **Some possible sources of radiation**

CASE STUDY – SUNBEDS

The British Medical Association wants people to be informed of the true risks of sunbeds. One of the myths of tanning is that it is healthy for you. A suntan is not a sign of good health – it means that the skin has been damaged by the sun's ultra-violet radiation.

This damage results in looking old early and increases your risk of getting skin cancer.

1 What are your views on the use of sunbeds?

2 How could you persuade people to stop using sunbeds?

Health and hygiene at work

Health and hygiene are not only important on a personal level, but are vital in the working environment. Hygiene is especially important for people working in a leisure organisation with catering facilities as they are working with food that customers will eat. For staff working in sports environments cleanliness and a healthy 'glow' can be important too.

GIVE IT A GO: food hygiene

The Food Hygiene Act 1990 is the legislation that supports food preparation and serving at work.

Find out what the Food Hygiene Act 1990 says about preparing and serving food at work. You could ask your canteen or kitchen staff, or you could log onto the Food Standards Agency website – a link is available at www.heinemann.co.uk/hotlinks (express code 0005P).

● *Personal cleanliness* ●

For anybody in a job that includes contact with other people, a good standard of personal hygiene and cleanliness is essential.

...a member of staff turned up for work...

- smelling of alcohol and smoke
- wearing paint-stained clothing
- with dirty hands and finger nails
- unshaved and with dirty uncombed hair
- with a painful looking skin condition on their hands and face?

With a partner, discuss how you would react if staff at a theatre, restaurant or health club did any of above?

Discuss why personal cleanliness is important personally and in a work environment.

● *General healthcare policies for employees* ●

Most organisations will have a healthcare code of practice or policy which must be followed. Large organisations also often have a health and safety officer who can give advice on standards of health or workplace conditions, such as an occupational nurse or someone to check that your computer is at the correct height etc.

If you feel you are working in an unhealthy environment, such as a smoky or dusty atmosphere, then you are allowed to ask for a health check or working environment check. In the sport and leisure industry this can mean checking for:

- *poorly ventilated or heated rooms and offices*
- *desks at the wrong height for computer work*
- *appropriate lifting gear for carrying heavy equipment*
- *noise from machinery*
- *flashing or faulty lights*
- *poor staff facilities – no washroom or showers.*

● *Private health insurance* ●

Some employees have a private health insurance policy, which can be provided by their employer. If they become chronically ill or have an accident they will be able to afford treatment through their policy. Private health insurance can be expensive but if you have a family history of problems or a job which exposes you to health risks it may be worth the cost.

GIVE IT A GO: health and hygiene

Choose a place where you would like to work, for example a theme park, sport centre, public swimming pool or holiday resort.

1 Working in small groups, write a list of the common health and hygiene difficulties you could find in your chosen workplace.

2 Write up any solutions your group can think of that may solve these problems.

Use a software package to present your thoughts to the rest of the class.

Alternative methods of transport

In this section you will look at what you and other people can do to help reduce atmospheric pollution. Using alternative methods of transport can also help to keep you healthy while you travel to and from work.

We shall look at:

▷ *personal means of transport*
▷ *public transport*
▷ *measures to improve transport.*

● *Personal means of transport* ●

This idea probably makes you think of a car, but this would not be the case in poorer countries where people are more likely to get around on foot, by bicycle or moped. In developed countries we have come to rely heavily on our cars. This, however, has a high cost for us and the environment: cars are expensive to buy and run; they burn precious fuels and create congestion. Overall they are not a very energy-efficient form of personal transport.

Walking
Walking is currently the UK's most popular form of leisure activity. The popular Ramblers Association (a link is available at www.heinemann.co.uk/hotlinks, express code 0005P) has a large membership for whom they organise walking day trips, holidays and outings throughout Britain. However, many people in Britain see walking as only a leisure activity and fewer and fewer people walk to work. Walking to work, school or college not only helps the environment but it can help you stay fit and healthy.

▲ Many people see walking as only a leisure activity

...I walked to college or school?

With a group of your friends make a pact to walk to college or school for two weeks. If you live too far away, try to walk part of the way – get off the bus two stops earlier, or walk to the train station from your house.

At the end of the week, discuss how you felt. Do you feel healthier? How do you think walking to work can help the environment?

Cycling

Cycling to work is less common than walking, but has even greater health benefit. Some companies encourage staff to cycle to work by providing changing rooms and secure bike sheds. In areas where there is a lot of traffic, people may choose to cycle to work to avoid sitting in traffic jams – they can sometimes get to work faster than people who drive! The disadvantages of cycling in traffic are the high levels of air pollution that you will be exposed to and the risk of being hit by a car.

▲ Cycling to work avoids sitting in a traffic jam

GIVE IT A GO: getting to work

Discuss with two others why cycling and walking to work are less popular today. Create a display board showing your reasons.

Driving

Driving to work has boomed. Car ownership has increased so much, that it now takes a long time and is very frustrating to get to work on time, especially during peak travelling times.

GIVE IT A GO: driving to work

1 Divide your class into two groups. In one group discuss what the advantages of using a car to get to work are. In the second group discuss the disadvantages of driving to work.

2 Try to debate the arguments.

Public transport

Public transport is promoted as the best alternative to driving. There are many advantages for individuals and the environment. For example:

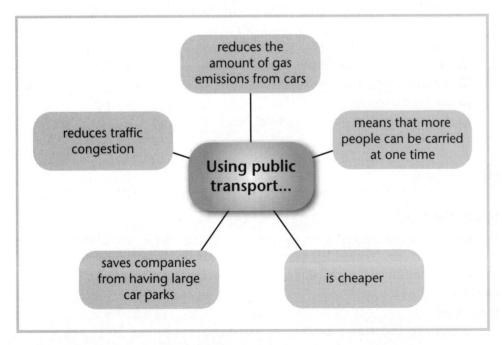

▲ **Some advantages of using public transport**

Some of the disadvantages of using public transport are:

- *buses are often slow, late and can also get caught in traffic congestion*
- *the underground is crowded and smelly*
- *travelling late at night on public transport can be dangerous*
- *there are limited public transport options at night.*

GIVE IT A GO: public transport

1 Think of two more advantages and two more disadvantages to add to the lists above. Compare your ideas with a partner.

2 Why do you think public transport seems to work better elsewhere than in the UK?

Measures to improve transport

The UK transport authorities work hard to offer alternative types of transport. The following are examples of where their work has been a success:

- *Sheffield's super tram*
- *new underground routes for the London underground system e.g. the Jubilee line*
- *new pedestrian areas and bridges that encourage walking and exclude traffic e.g. London and Newcastle's Millennium bridges, Oxford's Cornmarket street*
- *national cycle routes and cyclist-only lanes*
- *car-sharing lanes for busy commuter routes*
- *London's congestion charging zone*
- *new toll motorways*
- *fuel combination public transport buses.*

WHAT if?

...it keeps going on like this?

The earth has been warming since the Ice Age, but very, very slowly. Since the industrial revolution, the pace of change has increased considerably. The 1990s was the warmest decade since records began and 2003 was the third hottest year on record. The UK saw temperatures soar to 32°C at Gravesend in August 2003.

Are we to blame? If so, how?

EVIDENCE ACTIVITY  **P1**

Environmental factors

1 Select a job that you would like to do.

2 Explain the environmental factors that would be important to you if you were to do that job.

The law at work

At work you should always be treated fairly, bosses and colleagues should have **ethical practices** and you should set high standards for your work. In reality people are exploited, illegal practices go on and standards of work or quality of goods can be low. This is why we have laws.

How the law helps you at work

Remember that usually the law is on your side. The law ensures that decent standards, honest practices and ethical dealings are actually applied. Where they are not, people go to court to have them put right, be compensated for the wrongs and the culprits can be punished.

> **GLOSSARY**
>
> **Ethical practices** are fair and honest ways of working.

The benefits of following the law are:	The consequences of not following the law might be:
• the organisation and its staff meets their legal obligations • accidents are reduced • a clean, safe working environment is maintained • the environment benefits • customers and staff are happier • the organisation's reputation and image are good.	• closure of company • fines • bad publicity in the press • customers and staff leaving • frequent insurance claims • costs to clean up and repair damaged property or equipment if accident happens.

▲ The benefits of following the law and consequences of not following the law

Regulations and laws come from three sources:

▭ *Acts of Parliament – laws set out by the government*
▭ *outcomes of previous court cases – rulings made by judges*
▭ *the European Union – directives and regulations.*

● *Acts of Parliament* ●

Acts of Parliament are regularly being updated and the most important legislation that affects sport and leisure organisations is the Health and Safety at Work Act, 1974 (HASAWA) – see page 121 for more information on the 1992 version of this Act. Acts of Parliament are written to cover broad situations and to guide the behaviour of staff and companies. They are enforced by special organisations, for example HASAWA is enforced by the Health and Safety Executive (HSE), local authorities and even the police if necessary.

If a sport or leisure organisation breaks the law, they may be stopped by the police, closed by the local authority and investigated by the HSE. This investigation might result in a fine or, in serious cases, imprisonment.

● *Case law or common law* ●

Case law or common law are laws that are decided in court by judges. These decisions then become precedents (set the standard) for future cases. This means that if a similar case comes to court, then the judge will use the precedent to make a decision in the new case. Barristers can then refer to these decisions when defending or prosecuting cases, as you may have seen in many courtroom dramas on TV.

● *EU regulations* ●

EU regulations come from the European Parliament and apply to all countries who are part of the EU. These regulations often become important parts of the UK's Acts of Parliament.

Many EU regulations relevant to work date from 1992 and cover the following (all of which apply to the sport and leisure industry in some way):

- *Health and Safety and Welfare in the workplace*
- *Manual Handling Operations*
- *Personal Protective Clothing*
- *Use of Display Screen Equipment.*

EVIDENCE ACTIVITY

Work-related laws

1 Choose a job that interests you and create a chart that shows which laws are most important to that job. **P2**

2 Explain why some of these work-related laws are more important than others.   **P3**

Health and Safety at Work Act 1992

As you have learnt, HASAWA is the law which applies most to sport and leisure. Let us look at the issues that are covered in this law.

HASAWA covers:

- *working hours*
- *breaks*
- *minimum temperatures*
- *lighting*.

• *Working hours* •

The Act sets out maximum number of hours that you can safely work. This makes sure you are not expected to work too many hours, which could put your or other people's safety or welfare at risk. Another law that deals with the amount of hours you are allowed to work is called the Working Time Regulation.

• *Breaks* •

The Act also sets out how many breaks you need and how long each one needs to be to have a positive effect. This helps keep up your motivation and concentration, which could be important if you were lifeguarding in a busy pool, for example.

• *Minimum temperatures* •

A minimum temperature for workplaces is maintained for comfort and health. If the temperature falls below this level then you can stop work or ask for additional heating.

• *Lighting* •

Standards are set for lighting to make sure that employees' eyes are not strained and also to make sure that employees are safe, especially in corridors, store rooms and car parks.

In Unit 2, pages 36–37 you learnt that companies need to carry out a risk assessment to make sure that they meet the standards set out in HASAWA. Employers who are not following these standards can be prosecuted – just as you can for not following them!

• *Health and safety manuals* •

It is good practice to have a health and safety manual for all staff members to refer to. You should also be able to see a copy of the organisation's health and safety policy.

If you see any problems you must report them to your employer. If your employer does not fix them, you can call the HSE inspectors to test or check procedures.

The HSE inspectors have power to:

- ▷ *stop activities until action is taken to fix any problems*
- ▷ *serve an **improvement notice** for action to be taken quickly*
- ▷ *prosecute anyone breaking a law, which could result in a company's closure or even imprisonment of staff.*

Other laws at work

A range of other laws exist to help protect you and other staff at work. The following is an overview of some of the most common laws and how they apply to the sport and leisure industry.

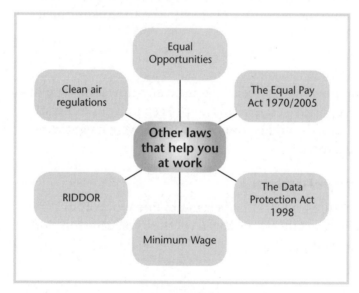

▲ Some of the more common laws

• *Equal Opportunities* •

Equal opportunities legislation is there to make sure you will be given the same chance as everyone else regardless of your gender, race, abilities, cultural or religious background. In sport and leisure this law supports you during the recruitment process, opportunities for promotion, opportunities to go on staff training programmes or making sure that disabled people have access to all facilities.

• *The Equal Pay Act 1970/2005* •

This law states that people doing the same job are entitled to the same pay, for example, women in the same role as men should be paid the same salary or wage.

> ### GLOSSARY
>
> An **Improvement notice** is an order made by a government agency that forces an organisation to make changes to improve safety.

The Data Protection Act 1998

This Act protects any personal information being held about you. The law stops information from being misused, for example, some companies sell their clients' contact details to marketing organisations and these organisations send you advertisements for products by mail, email or to your mobile phone. The Data Protection Act 1998 also gives you the right to see any information a company holds about you to check that it is accurate, such as your appraisal form or personnel records at work.

Minimum pay

The government sets **minimum pay** levels (£4.85 an hour in 2004). This can often be an issue for low-paid workers in the leisure industry who do not work full time, such as seasonal workers or casual labourers.

Reporting of Injuries, Diseases and Dangerous Occurrences Regulations (RIDDOR)

RIDDOR explains the legal way to report any injuries, diseases or dangerous occurrences that may happen in the workplace. In the sport and leisure industry this means reporting all accidents, illnesses, near misses (such as people falling in a sports centre), and equipment breakages, even if no one is hurt. All of these issues must be reported to ensure that they do not happen frequently.

Clean air

This legislation covers standards for the condition of air at work, which you looked at on page 114. In sport and leisure this might mean protection against poor air circulation and extraction from a swimming pool area.

> **GLOSSARY**
>
> **Minimum pay** is the smallest amount of money a company can pay its employees an hour.

GIVE IT A GO:

There are a number of other laws and standards supported by laws and regulations. Look at the following list and think of examples of where they would apply to the sport and leisure industry.

- **discrimination** – not making racist, sexist, ageist comments etc.
- meeting industry codes of practice with regard to young children
- First Aid regulations – up-to-date First Aid boxes and having qualified First Aiders on call
- certain permits are needed for sports and leisure facilities, such as licensing for alcohol, the number of people allowed at the facility at one time or gambling
- consumer and trading laws – these protect people who are selling products and people who are buying them

• *Best practice* •

In order to ensure that all laws are being upheld and that your organisation is a healthy and safe environment to work in, employers need to regularly train and update staff.

They might do this by:

- *holding training days on certain issues or new legislation*
- *sending staff to be trained by experts e.g. First Aid or lifesaving*
- *having experts come to the organisation to do demonstrations e.g. how to clean, carry and use equipment properly*
- *staging practice evacuation sessions e.g. for fire drills*
- *making sure that all staff have access to the proper documentation to report problems*
- *giving staff leaflets and brochures on new legislation*
- *role playing bad practice scenarios and how to deal with them.*

THINK ABOUT IT

Read the following scenarios and then answer the questions.

a Gill is a leisure centre duty manager. Every two days Gill does a round of checks. During one of her routine checks she spots the following:
  • the cleaning fluids cupboard has not been locked
  • the fire exit is blocked with sports bags
  • two First Aid boxes are missing.

b Sanjay works as an ice patrol person for a busy ice-skating rink. He sees a group of teenage boys racing across the ice. They are making a lot of noise and are disturbing the other skaters.

c You are a senior member of staff and the centre manager has asked you to lead a new staff induction programme focusing on health, safety and hygiene.

d You are a new member of staff at a popular holiday resort. You overhear a conversation in the staff changing room which includes some racist and sexist comments about customers.

1 Try to make a judgement on what the best action to take is for each of these short scenarios. Work with a partner and discuss with other groups after you have reached your solution.

2 Write five guidelines for dealing with a sports accident and design a form to record the details.

3 Find out what the basic contents of a First Aid box are and make a chart to illustrate them.

Find the answers to the questions in the puzzle. They could be written across, down or diagonally, backwards or forwards.

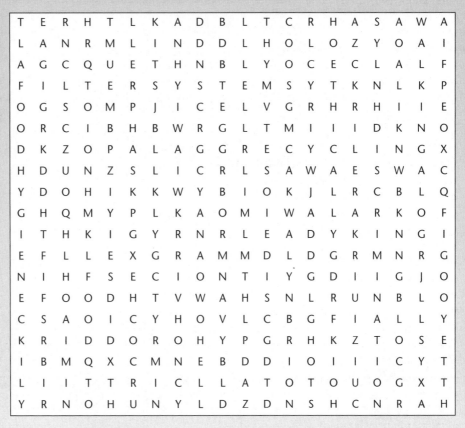

1 Re-using old materials is called . . .

2 What is another term for the greenhouse effect?

3 What is the word used to describe materials that decompose naturally?

4 They are used to control air quality in a sports facility.

5 Which Act governs the serving of food at a swimming pool café?

6 The healthiest way to get to work school or college?

7 The word for treating people fairly, honestly and equally.

8 The abbreviated form of the Health and Safety at Work Act.

9 A word used to describe treating people unfairly, badly or differently for no good reason.

10 The abbreviated form of Reporting of Injuries, Diseases and Dangerous Occurrences Regulations.

unit 6

Financial management

This unit will give you the knowledge and confidence to manage your own money. You will look at how money is earned and how to budget the money you earn. There are only Pass criteria available for this unit and there are six separate areas you need to produce evidence for.

This unit is internally assessed. This means, to pass this unit, you will complete an assignment set and marked by your tutor.

In this unit you will need to learn about:

▭ sources of income
▭ managing your personal finances
▭ the importance of keeping a personal budget.

Sources of income

Sources of income means all the ways in which we get money. For most people, there are three main sources of income: wages or salary from working, money from other places, such as interest on savings or money from the government that a person receives because he or she cannot work.

Income at work

For most people, their personal income comes from the job or jobs they have. As we have seen in Unit 1, pages 12–15, there are a number of different ways in which people earn money. These are:

▭ *being employed by another person or organisation as an employee (can be full- or part-time)*
▭ *working for yourself as a self-employed person*
▭ *working for yourself, but carrying out work for other people or organisations over a short period on a freelance basis.*

GIVE IT A GO: types of jobs

Make a list of the types of jobs where you are likely to be classed as:

• an employee
• self-employed
• freelance.

The income that you earn can be in the form of:

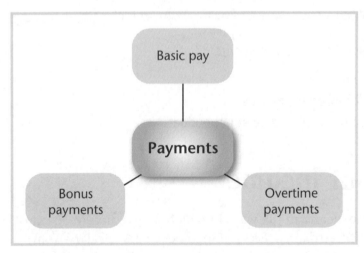

▲ Income can be in different forms

Basic pay

Your basic pay is the amount you are paid for doing a set number of hours in a week, as agreed in your contract. The number of hours will be based on whether you are a full- or part-time employee (see pages 12–16 for more information on types of jobs). If you are employed on a casual basis, then the amount you will earn per week will depend on the number of hours you have worked during that week.

Overtime payments

Overtime payments are paid when you complete extra hours of work. Extra hours are hours over and above the number agreed upon in your contract. Sometimes these are hours of work that are outside of your normal weekly requirement, like finishing at 6pm instead of 5pm, or starting at 7am instead of 8am. It may also mean working on an extra day or working during a public holiday, like Christmas. Remember that the sport and leisure industry often operates 24 hours a day, 7 days a week and over holidays. Your normal working hours and days may include these times and extra hours will be anything more than those agreed upon in your contract. This may be a part of your normal working week but you are paid at a different rate based on your hourly rate of pay. Double time, for instance, means that instead of £5 per hour, you are paid £10 per hour.

Bonus payments

Bonus payments are generally paid when a target has been achieved. For instance, if you work in a health club, you may receive a bonus payment every time you sign up a new club member (see pages 29 and 32 for more information on bonuses). This is sometimes called commission.

Self-employed and freelance workers

When you are self-employed or freelance, your income may not be as regular as when you work for an organisation, either full-time or part-time. Some weeks you may have a lot or work for which you are paid, while in other weeks you may have little or none at all! This can make budgeting more difficult. You will also need to organise paying your tax and other deductions yourself. However, as a freelancer or self-employed person, you set the price you will be paid, rather than someone else.

● *Gross and net pay* ●

You will come across the following two terms that refer to the money you have earned – gross and net pay. Gross pay is the total amount you have earned for the period of time in question – a week, or month, for example. It will include any bonus or overtime payments you may have earned. Net pay is the amount of money you will receive once all the **deductions** have been taken off. This is the amount that will actually go into your bank account.

> **GLOSSARY**
>
> **Deductions** are sums of money taken from your pay before you receive it, such as income tax or National Insurance.

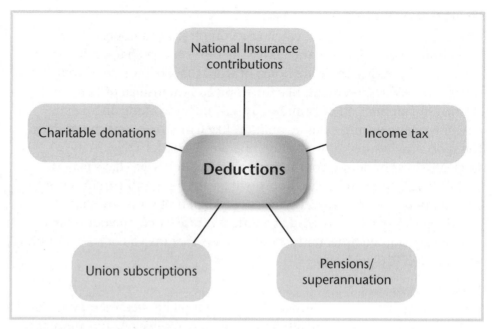

▲ Deductions that may be taken from your gross pay

Income tax and National Insurance

The two most common deductions are income tax and National Insurance. All employees who earn above a certain amount per year pay income tax. The money collected from income tax payment goes to the government to pay for a variety of public services – the police, health services like doctors and dentists or schools and colleges.

The amount of income tax that you pay is calculated as a certain percentage of your earnings each week or month. Some employees will pay more than others based on how much they earn. The more you earn – the more you will pay. Some employees do not pay income tax; they are exempt. For example, students in full-time education who have a job are exempt from paying income tax.

National Insurance is a payment that all employees have to make. Contributing to National Insurance means that, if necessary, you are able to claim the following allowances and benefits:

- *Jobseeker's Allowance*
- *Maternity Allowance*
- *Retirement Pension*
- *Widowed Parent's Allowance*
- *Bereavement Payment*
- *Bereavement Allowance*
- *Incapacity Benefit.*

Like income tax, the amount of money you pay toward National Insurance is based on how much money you earn. If you earn between £85 and £575 per week you will pay 10 percent of your earnings as a National Insurance contribution. In the pay advice slip on page 132, you can see that no National Insurance has been paid because the employee has not earned enough money. Your employer will also pay a similar amount towards your National Insurance contributions. Every time you claim sick pay or you become unemployed, your National Insurance contributions cover this. If you are self-employed or work freelance you will still need to make regular payments towards your National Insurance.

THINK ABOUT IT

Look at the list of allowances and benefits on page 133 that you can claim if you have paid National Insurance. In small groups, try to explain why these are necessary?

Pensions and superannuation

Another deduction that you will experience is called superannuation. This is a regular payment you will make to enable you to receive the state pension when you retire. Your working life is likely to be for at least 40 years so it is important that you make provision for when you are no longer able to work. Once you retire the state will pay you a pension each week, until you die. This currently stands at £79.60 per week. Women are currently entitled to a pension at the age of 60 while for men the age for a pension is 65. From 2020, a woman born after 5 April 1950 will also need to be 65 or over to receive the state pension.

You may also decide to make extra contributions towards your pension, known as additional voluntary contributions. These are a form of savings plan for your later years. It is important to remember that the earlier you start to save for your old age, the easier and more beneficial it will be.

Union subscriptions and charitable donations

Some employees may wish to join a trade union that will look after their interests. This means that they will have to pay a membership fee which will often be taken directly from their salary every month. Employees may wish to make a regular donation to a charity, Oxfam for example, and this can also be taken directly from their salary.

● *Pay advice slip* ●

As you have learnt from Unit 2 (pages 28–30), your income will be paid as a weekly wage or a monthly salary, which will be paid into your bank account. Very few people are paid in cash – wages and salaries are usually paid electronically into your bank account via a BACS payment.

To prove that the payment has been made your employer will give you a pay advice slip. This is a sheet detailing how much you have earned and what deductions have been made for things such as income tax and National Insurance.

Let us look at an example to make this easier to understand.

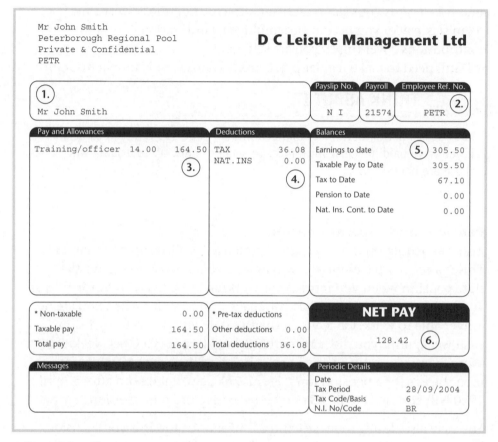

▲ **Pay advice slip**

On the above pay advice slip you can see a number of important pieces of information. They are:

1   the name of the employee

2   the employee reference number

3   the amount of money earned

4   the amount of income tax and National Insurance paid

5   a **summary of earnings** to the current date

6   how much money has been paid to the employee for the work carried out.

GLOSSARY

Summary of earnings is a description of all the money that a person has earned over a period of time – a week, a month or a year.

Other sources of income

Apart from the actual money you earn from your job, you may be entitled to further payments to supplement your income, especially if you are classed as being on a low income.

• *Allowances and benefits* •

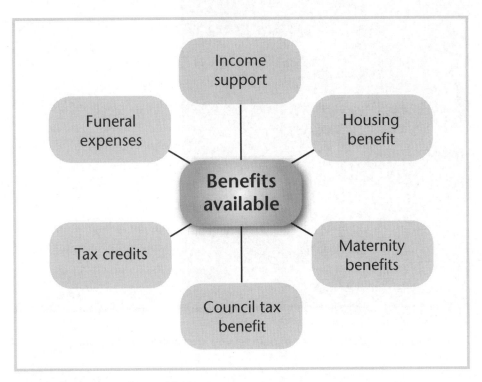

▲ **Benefits you may be entitled to**

There are a number of benefits available to people living and working in the United Kingdom. For example, if you earn below a certain amount per week, the council tax you need to pay may be reduced. How much you earn will affect the benefits that you are allowed to claim, this is called **means testing**. Your income is taken into account when calculating how much of a particular benefit you are entitled to.

Benefits may be available to you if you:

- *have dependent children*
- *are sick or disabled*
- *are caring for someone who is unable to earn an income*
- *are aged 60 or over*
- *are pregnant or have recently had a baby*
- *are on a low income.*

▲ You may be entitled to claim benefits if you are caring for someone

These benefits are designed to support people bringing up a family, to ensure everybody has a decent **standard of living** and to provide help when things go wrong.

WHAT if?

...I need financial help?

1 Choose three different reasons why you might need financial help.

2 Log onto the Department for Works and Pensions website – a link is available at www.heinemann.co.uk/hotlinks (express code 0005P) and find out what help is available.

3 Produce a leaflet, which tells people about this help. Remember to include any conditions that apply, such as level of income.

• *Saving, inheriting and borrowing money* •

You may find that there are other sources of income that become available to you when you start work apart from the income from the job itself and any state benefits to which you are entitled.

If you have money saved in a bank account then the bank will pay **interest** to you as a reward for using that bank. Current accounts are suitable for everyday use and you will earn interest on the amount of money left in the account. There are special accounts designed for saving money. These are called deposit accounts and will pay a higher rate of interest. The more money you have in the account, the more interest you will earn.

You may also inherit money, for example if a relative or parent were to pass away and left you money in their will. Finally, you may decide that you wish to borrow money from a bank or building society to buy a car, carry out home improvements or even buy a home. You will pay back the borrowed amount, plus interest, a little bit each month.

> **GLOSSARY**
>
> **Interest** is the amount of money you receive every year because you have invested your money in a bank or building society.

Income when you are out of work

Unfortunately some people are unable to keep a job due to illness or disability. Some people cannot find a job due to high unemployment. As a result some of the benefits you have looked at are not available. So what help is there for people who do not have a job? Some of the benefits you can claim are:

- *Jobseeker's Allowance*
- *Income Support*
- *Child Benefit*
- *Housing Benefit.*

GIVE IT A GO: what benefits are available for the unemployed?

1 Complete the following table for a range of benefits. An example has been done for you.

Benefit	Who can claim this?	What conditions apply?	How much money is paid?	Comments
Jobseeker's Allowance	People who do not have jobs. You must be over 18.	You must be available for work		You may still be able to work part-time, as long as work is less than 16 hours per week
Income Support				
Child Benefit				
Housing Benefit				

EVILENCE ACTIVITY

Earning money for a trip

1 You have decided to go on the trip of a lifetime next summer with your friends from school or college. The only problem is how to pay for it!

   a In small groups, list as many different ways you could earn money from a job in the sport and leisure sector.

   b Choose **one** job and look at the different ways, such as overtime, that money can be earned.

   c What **other** sources of income are available to pay for this trip?

2 Get a payslip from either your parents (preferable) or one of your own (if there is no other example available) from a part-time job you have. Look at all the information on the payslip and explain what it is. Describe the income and deductions to your teacher on a one-to-one basis.

Managing your personal finances

Learning how to manage your finances is a very important part of earning money. Planning what you spend your hard-earned income on and when, will ensure that you do not run out of money before you are next paid. Many people worry a lot about money and money problems can be a cause of great stress. By following some very simple steps and by being careful and organised you can avoid making the mistakes that lead to money problems.

▲ **Budgeting will ensure you do not run out of money before pay day**

GIVE IT A GO: how much do you spend?

1 Make a list of all the things you spend money on each week, for example, your mobile phone, clothes, savings, bills and entertainment.

2 Add the amounts together and compare your list with six other people in your class. How do you compare?

Attitudes to work and money

It is often said that you can only spend your money once! The way you view money, or your **attitude** towards your money, will affect how easy you find it to manage the income you bring home each week or month.

• *What attitude do you have?* •

There are many different attitudes to money. The attitude you have will have an effect on your **spending habits**. Some people are savers – they like to 'save for a rainy day'. Savers will put money aside each month to make sure they have enough money to pay for unexpected essential things like car repairs or new bicycle tyres.

Some people are spenders – they 'live for today'. Spenders want to buy things now and don't think about what money they may need tomorrow. Some spenders have a weakness for certain items, like shoes or CDs, and cannot resist a bargain!

▲ **Some people cannot resist a bargain!**

◯ THINK ABOUT IT

What is your attitude to money? Do you save? Do you gamble – this could include buying tickets for the lottery, playing bingo or betting on a horse or greyhound race? What do you spend your money on? What do you feel about having a credit card?

GIVE IT A GO: attitudes to money

1 As a class, discuss your different attitudes to money and how you spend it.
2 See if you can find a newspaper article about people in debt. What are the consequences of allowing this to happen?

• *What lifestyle do you expect?* •

Your spending will be affected by your attitude to money as well as your hopes and aspirations. A person who is planning on getting married may try to save as much as he or she can. A young single person, on the other hand, may feel happy to spend all his or her money and not worry about what might happen tomorrow.

What is more important to you? Working in a job that you really enjoy regardless of how much you get paid? Or is it just the amount of money you earn that is the most important factor? For some people a job is simply a way of earning money to pay for the lifestyle they want or expect. Many lifestyles, such as David and Victoria Beckham's, need lots of money to maintain – luckily for them David Beckham earns a lot of money!

▲ **David Beckham has a lifestyle that many people would like to have**

Using banks, building societies and post offices

There are many sources of help available to help you manage your personal finances. These include banks, building societies, post offices and insurance companies. The help they can provide comes in many forms. Look at the following example.

CASE STUDY – THE NORWICH AND PETERBOROUGH BUILDING SOCIETY

The Norwich and Peterborough Building Society is a large banking organisation, which offers a range of services that could help you look after your money. The society offers its customers:

- a range of bank accounts, both savings and current
- advice on a range of insurance products
- a chance to buy and sell stocks and shares
- other ways of investing money for the future, such as **ISA**s
- a range of personal and business loans
- mortgages for buying a house or flat.

The society has a number of branches around the country, mainly in the eastern part of the country. The society also offers an Internet banking service for people who have Internet access and are unable to visit a branch during normal banking hours.

Staff at the bank can offer help and guidance over a range of financial matters like savings and making investments – making your money work for you. If you can leave a balance of money in your account at the end of each month, you will earn interest on this money.

Log onto the Norwich and Peterborough Building Society website – a link is available at www.heinemann.co.uk/hotlinks (express code 0005P).

1 Research the ways it can help you with your money and finances.

2 Produce a chart which highlights all the services and products it has that would help you when you start working.

3 Compare the interest rates offered for both a savings and a current account. Which account offers the best rate of interest?

Running a bank or building society account

When you open a bank account, you will need to learn how to:

- *use a cheque book*
- *use a cheque guarantee card*
- *read statements on your account*
- *use a debit and/or credit card.*

• *Cheque books* •

A cheque is a written instruction to your bank to pay an amount of money to another person. Look at the cheque below to see what information is required on a cheque.

Star Bank

08-60-81

Peterborough Business Park, Lynch Wood, Peterborough PE2 6WZ

Date

Pay _____ only

the sum of _____

ACCOUNT PAYEE

£ _____

20/09/04
This cheque contains a watermark
and other Security Features designed to prevent fraud

Mr. J. Smith

_____
Signatures

12345678 086081

▲ **An example of a blank cheque**

A cheque must always include the following:

1 a **bank sort code**

2 an account name and number

3 who the cheque is payable to

4 a space where the amount to be paid is written in words

5 a space where the amount is written in numbers

6 a space for the date

7 a space for the account holder to sign.

All of these things must be on the cheque for it to be valid. If you make a mistake while writing out a cheque, you must sign next to the error, if you are the account holder. The cheque must also always be signed by the account or cheque holder and the date must be included.

• *Cheque guarantee card* •

When you pay by cheque, you will be asked to show your cheque guarantee card. This is a plastic card that has a special number and the cheque holder's signature on it. The shop or person receiving the cheque can then make sure that the cheque is yours and is not **fraudulent**. The cheque card number will then be written on the back of the cheque and means the payment is guaranteed up to either £50 or £100, depending on the card presented.

> **GLOSSARY**
>
> **Bank sort code** is a six-digit code that identifies a particular branch of bank or building society.

> **GLOSSARY**
>
> **Fraudulent** is when someone tries to get money by being dishonest.

WHAT if?

...*my cheque bounces?*

Phone your local bank and find out what happens when a cheque is not accepted by a retailer. Do you think cheques are an efficient way to make payments? Discuss this with members of your class.

• *Debit and credit cards* •

Debit cards are being used more frequently as they can be used to pay for items directly. Instead of writing a cheque, the card can be swiped through an electronic machine that reads the information stored on your card. The machine links up to your bank to check if you have enough money in your account and if the card is valid. If it is not then your payment will be denied. If your card is accepted, you then sign a sales document, or more frequently enter your PIN, and the money spent is taken directly from your bank account.

Credit cards operate in a similar way: once the card has been swiped and accepted, you have bought the items. The main difference is that you can use a credit card to pay for goods even if you don't have the money in your account. Your credit card company will lend you the money, but you must pay it back. At the end of the month you will receive a bill for the total amount you have spent on that card. You can choose to pay either the whole bill or part of it by a certain date. If the whole bill is not paid, your bank will charge you interest on the amount outstanding. The rate of interest is usually very high compared to other ways of borrowing money.

▲ Debit cards are replacing cash and cheques as a way to pay for goods and services

Personal finance records

If you operate a bank account or a credit card, you will receive a statement every month. Your statement shows all the **transactions** that you have made on your account for that month. Your bank account statement will show:

▭ *all payments made into and out of your account*
▭ *the date of all monthly payments, such as gas and electricity*
▭ *any charges made by your bank, such as interest on borrowings or charges for being overdrawn*
▭ *the amount of money you had at the start of the month and the amount you had at the end, also called your opening and closing balances.*

All transactions shown on your statement will have the date on which they occurred.

A credit card statement is similar. It will show:

▭ *the details of all transactions made on the card including purchases and payments*
▭ *the opening and closing balance for the card*
▭ *the minimum amount you have to pay back to the bank and the date before which the payment must to be paid*
▭ *the amount of interest charged on the outstanding balance.*

It is very important to read your statements carefully. Everyone can make mistakes, even banks! If you do not check your statements you may not notice any errors. Be warned: if you miss the payment date on a credit card, your bank will charge you a large fee as a penalty!

● *Internet and telephone banking* ●

Nowadays, the option of banking at home using the Internet is becoming very popular, especially for people who are unable to visit their bank during normal working hours. You can log onto your bank's website and check up-to-date statements, get account information and make payments. Some people also do most of their shopping over the Internet as it is fast and easy. There is still some concern about how secure Internet banking or shopping is. As technology improves, this way of managing your money should become increasingly safe to use.

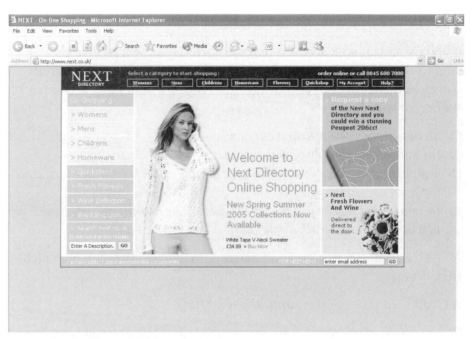

▲ Some people do most of their shopping over the Internet

Many banks also have a telephone service that is available 24 hours a day to allow customers to check balances, pay bills and complete other financial transactions.

EVIDENCE ACTIVITY

A personal budget

1 Following on from the previous assessment activity, you now need to **plan** your spending over the next few weeks and months to ensure that you have sufficient money to pay for the holiday and provide spending money, money for food and drink, and so on. **P3**

  a Draw up a **personal budget** for the next few weeks to ensure that you have your finances under control.

  b Identify all the spending being made and the **income** coming in.

  c What are you able to save **regularly**? Will this pay for the holiday? If not, how will you change your budget?

2 Draw up a plan for managing your personal finance over the next few months to ensure you are able to go on this holiday. Include a weekly budget for your income and spending for the next six weeks. Discuss this with your teacher or whoever else will monitor your budget with you. **P4**

Using and keeping a budget

Using a personal budget plan is very important if you are to avoid getting into financial trouble. You cannot spend what you do not have! Managing your personal finances with the help of a budget will make sure that all your bills are planned for and that you have money to enjoy a social life with your friends and family.

Personal budgeting

Keeping a budget means working out how much money you will need each week or month. Planning a personal budget can be quite complicated. You will need to include all your bills and **expenses** you have for the week or month, so that you do not spend more money than you earn. You also need to make sure that you have enough money to pay for large bills, like your road tax for your car. When keeping a budget, it is important that you list all money coming in and all the payments going out.

• *Why budget?* •

The benefits of budgeting are:

◘ *making sure that money is available to pay all your bills and other outgoings*
◘ *large bills that are due at a particular time are planned for*
◘ *you ensure that you do not spend more money than you have available.*

By not budgeting, you risk going **overdrawn** at your bank or building society – you will have to pay large charges for this. Other problems could include cheques that bounce because you do not have enough money in your account or other regular payments (telephone line rental, house or flat rent) not being made.

> **GLOSSARY**
>
> **Expenses** refer to the costs of things you need to do in everyday life. If you have expenses while doing your job, you can often get your company to pay for these – taking a customer out to lunch, for example.

> **GLOSSARY**
>
> **Overdrawn** is when your bank account has a negative balance: you have taken out too much money and you now owe the bank.

EVIDENCE ACTIVITY

Why budget?

1 In small groups, make a list of all the benefits you can think of for keeping a budget.

2 Now list the problems you may find if you fail to keep a close check on you money.

3 In your groups, discuss why you think managing your personal finances is important.

Planning your budget

There are many factors to think about when you are planning your budget. The diagram below shows some of the essential factors that must be included in any budget that you plan.

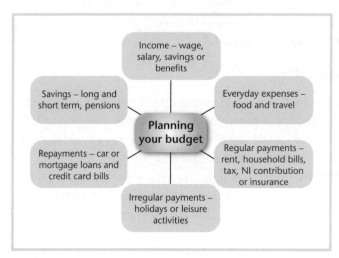

▲ There are many things you need to plan for in your budget

CASE STUDY – WILLIAMS FAMILY BUDGET

The following is the Williams family's weekly budget.

Income	
Mr Williams' weekly take home pay	£370.00
Mrs Williams' weekly take home pay	£ 80.00
Child benefit	£ 25.00
Expenditure	
Food	£ 85.00
Mortgage repayment	£155.00
Council tax	£ 11.27
Water rates	£ 6.15
Electricity and gas	£ 17.00
Insurance for car and house	£ 22.00
Car repayment	£ 75.00
Household items	£ 10.00
Telephone bill	£ 14.00
Clothes for family	£ 35.00
Entertainment	£ 55.00
Television licence	£ 2.00
Children's pocket money	£ 20.00

1 What is the balance at the end of each month? Are they in credit or debt and by how much?

2 Which areas of spending are essential – they cannot do without these items?

3 Suggest how they might change their current budget. Consider both income and expenditure when doing this.

4 What other sources of help or income are available to the Williams family? Give two examples.

• *Long-term planning* •

Although you will plan a weekly or a monthly budget, depending on whether you earn a wage or a salary, it is important that you look at how much money you will need over a longer time period. This means planning ahead for payments you know you will have to pay in the future. For example, if you drive a car your road tax is payable every 6 or 12 months. You should allow a certain amount *each* month so you have saved enough money to pay when it is next due. If you drive a small car, your road tax might be £110. You can save £10 each month over a year towards this future bill. You might save this money in a bank or building society or even buy car tax stamps each week or month from the post office. This is an example of planning your budget.

IF ONLY I HAD SAVED SOME MONEY FOR MY ROAD TAX!

▲ **Make sure you plan for long-term payments!**

EVIDENCE ACTIVITY  P6

Produce a personal budget plan

1 Plan your personal budget. Use the table below to help you by filling in your current income and spending. Be honest! Include everything that you spend money on – food and drink, entertainment, regular spending such as rent, insurance, gas and electricity etc. Remember it is easier to work out everything the same as the way you are paid – either weekly or monthly.

When you draw up your budget, remember to include:

- irregular payments – entertainment, holidays etc.
- repayments – car or house loans, credit card bills etc.
- any savings plans that you have – pensions or deposit account.

Income		Expenditure	
Source	Amount (£)	Source	Amount (£)
For example, – wage from leisure centre – overtime – bonus payments		For example, – food and rent to parents – mobile phone bill – car tax – car insurance – road tax – going out – match fees for football – travel – holiday – entertainment	

2 Now check whether your budget is balanced. Are you in credit or debt and by how much?

3 Make a list of all the ways that you can improve your budget.

Find the answers to the questions in the puzzle. They could be written across, down or diagonally, backwards or forwards.

M	E	G	C	H	B	F	B	I	E	D	B	O	B	A	N	K	A	C	C	O	U	N	T
E	A	M	E	O	L	E	J	L	X	M	F	N	V	K	K	D	X	N	A	T	R	D	M
A	U	R	M	Q	A	T	N	L	C	H	N	I	W	E	P	G	T	I	O	N	F	I	T
N	B	N	P	T	C	Y	V	E	R	Z	K	N	I	G	R	O	S	S	I	P	N	F	U
S	M	A	L	I	K	D	G	H	F	F	E	C	G	N	E	O	T	S	C	M	I	E	W
T	D	T	O	O	A	O	L	F	I	F	U	C	L	G	D	I	H	A	Z	N	H	M	H
E	V	F	Y	N	I	N	S	L	A	R	T	G	E	F	F	B	E	M	K	A	I	G	M
S	N	P	E	I	A	W	K	Z	N	K	J	S	D	A	J	H	M	G	E	L	N	P	B
T	K	H	E	T	J	B	I	L	L	S	X	I	E	Z	N	E	X	I	I	L	T	T	U
I	Z	C	A	L	N	N	A	T	I	O	N	A	L	I	N	S	U	R	A	N	C	E	D
N	A	O	U	F	L	P	H	U	K	C	R	F	Q	U	F	L	H	C	O	J	L	E	X
G	K	P	A	Y	A	D	V	I	C	E	G	E	B	U	D	Y	L	L	B	D	I	K	B
H	D	X	E	P	B	P	K	M	B	H	Y	E	T	E	J	X	E	I	E	U	K	N	J
P	G	D	C	H	I	L	D	B	E	N	E	F	I	T	K	H	B	V	N	F	D	Y	T
E	S	K	J	Y	N	O	D	O	I	N	G	S	D	G	I	D	M	A	R	I	S	B	K
N	I	N	G	A	E	S	E	L	F	E	M	P	L	O	Y	E	D	Z	Q	N	M	U	N
S	M	E	E	I	E	O	O	C	V	L	G	H	B	W	I	V	C	F	L	S	T	D	B
C	L	G	J	I	N	T	M	B	H	T	T	A	N	J	N	K	H	O	K	G	I	G	L
I	N	T	E	R	E	S	T	R	F	A	G	D	U	C	K	Z	A	L	H	S	O	E	C
Q	I	K	C	H	N	B	P	J	E	X	P	E	N	D	I	T	U	R	E	E	N	T	I

1 When you get a job you will be an _____.

2 When you work for yourself you are _____.

3 Payment for extra hours worked is called _____.

4 The piece of paper you get which tells you about how much you have earned is your _____ slip.

5 Your earnings **before** deductions are taken off are known as your _____ pay.

6 _____ is one of the deductions taken from you wages or salary at source.

7 Payments from the government to people who are experiencing difficulties are known as _____.

8 The method used to calculate your entitlement to benefits is called _____.

9 _____ is a source of income which comes from banks or building societies.

10 A payment you receive if you have children is _____.

11 To make sure you do not run out of money, you need to keep to a _____.

12 When you open a _____, you will get a cheque book.

13 If your have money left over at the end of the week or month, you are in the _____.

14 The opposite of income is _____.

15 _____ have to be paid when they arrive!

unit 7

Organising a sport or leisure event

In this unit you will find out about a wide range of different events held in the sport and leisure industry. You will also look at the different skills you will need to be able to organise an event yourself, and the range of resources that might be needed to ensure an event is a success. You will need to plan an event including thinking about the type of event, who the event is for, resources and health and safety issues. Finally, you will also take part in organising an actual event, commenting on how the event went and the part you played in its success.

This unit is internally assessed. This means, to pass this unit, you will complete an assignment set and marked by your tutor.

In this unit you will need to learn about:

▷ a range of different types of sport and leisure events
▷ the skills and resources needed to organise and deliver an event
▷ planning a sport or leisure event
▷ taking part in the organisation and delivery of a sport or leisure event.

Types of sport and leisure events

In Unit 1 we looked at what was meant by the words sport and leisure (read pages 2–3 again to remind you). A leisure event is one that people will go to in their spare time: an exhibition, a motor show or a car boot sale. A sports event is more specific and refers to things like a football match, a golf tournament or a marathon.

The size of a sport and leisure event can vary, from thousands of people attending an international football match or a national exhibition, to only a few attending a local pub's dart competition or the village bridge players' summer barbeque.

Sport events

Sport events are usually competitive where players take part in the event while **spectators** watch it. A sport event can take place indoors or outdoors. The players can be in teams, such as football or hockey, or they can compete individually, like darts or swimming. There are always rules and regulations which players must obey, even in an **endurance event**.

Leisure events

Most leisure events involve less competitive activities such as car boot sales, fêtes and fashion shows. Like sport events they can take place indoors or outdoors. A leisure event can include visits and trips to places of historical, cultural or local interest, for example, a trip to the Scottish Border region to visit houses built in the 17th century. Many leisure events are held in order to raise money for special causes – some country estates may open their gardens to visitors during the summer to raise money for a charitable cause.

▲ **Car boot sales are a popular leisure event**

EVICENCE ACTIVITY

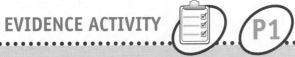

P1

Types of sport and leisure events

1 Use the clues to find different types of sport and leisure activities in the word search below.

1 Designers show off their new clothes at a…? (7, 4 letters).

2 The FA… final? (3 letters).

3 Arsenal and Manchester United play in the Premier…? (6 letters).

4 A … cricket, football and rugby tournament happens every four years. (5, 3 letters).

5 A sports event where you all play everyone at least once. (5, 5 letters).

6 You buy a ticket and the winner is often pulled from a hat to win a prize. (6 letters).

7 Many pubs will hold general knowledge … night. (4 letters).

8 People try to sell their unwanted goods at a …. (3, 4, 4 letters).

9 A school will hold a summer … to raise money. (4 letters).

10 In squash, you might play in one of these to climb up the rankings. (6 letters).

11 Another name for a show where you can listen to live music. (7 letters).

12 The NEC in Birmingham and the Tate in London hold these. (11 letters).

F	A	S	H	I	O	N	S	H	O	W	X	R
E	C	A	R	B	O	O	T	S	A	L	E	O
T	W	V	T	P	O	K	M	E	C	U	J	U
E	D	M	D	P	G	L	Q	F	S	Q	R	N
Q	B	R	I	G	N	A	N	D	Y	U	B	D
T	Z	C	A	J	W	J	L	C	P	I	W	R
C	U	P	R	L	B	Q	C	A	Y	Z	C	O
V	C	L	E	A	G	U	E	L	K	P	B	B
E	A	F	M	D	O	F	W	D	C	Y	A	I
W	O	R	L	D	C	U	P	F	K	I	U	N
C	O	N	C	E	R	T	B	Z	I	Z	C	R
S	A	B	D	R	A	F	F	L	E	T	Q	M
R	E	X	H	I	B	I	T	I	O	N	S	I

2 Copy out and complete the table below, giving examples of team and individual sport and leisure events. Try to get ten examples in each box.

	Individual	Team
Sport events	Beat-the-keeper	Cricket World Cup
Leisure events	White Elephant sale	Trip to the seaside

Skills and resources

In order to organise an event successfully, you will need both skills and resources. Skills are things you can do or are good at, for example communicating with people, using numbers or using a computer. Resources are any materials, equipment or things you might need for the event. For example, if you are organising a beat-the-keeper game for a school fête you will need a goal with a net, a marked-out shooting area, some balls and, of course, a goalkeeper.

Skills

There are many types of skills that will be useful when organising an event. Each person's skills are known as their personal skills and skills that the whole team have are known as team skills. Look at the following skills:

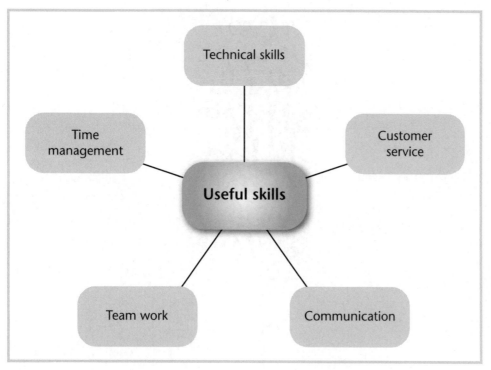

▲ **Skills used in organising an event**

● *Team work skills* ●

Team work is probably the most important skill that everyone involved in organising an event should have. Not everyone in every team needs to have the same skills, but they do need to be able to pull their different skills together so that they can make the event successful. This is known as team work. For example, a person with good organisational skills can be in charge of the team, a person with good technical skills can make sure all the equipment works and someone with communication skills can do all the talking to customers.

It is important then that every team member knows what **role** they are going to play in making sure the event is a success. If people cannot work together and all 'pull in the same direction', then team members will work against each other instead of helping each other.

GLOSSARY

A **role** is what a person is expected to do. For example, a lifeguard is expected to help a swimmer who is having trouble in the water.

▲ This tug-of-war team will be successful because they are working together

● *Customer care skills* ●

Most events include lots of people other than the organisers. Customer care skills are skills that involve looking after these people. For example, on a trip to the seaside for a group of pensioners, making sure that every-one is happy, comfortable, not hungry or tired, or simply having a conversation with some of them, are all customer care skills.

● *Communication skills* ●

Some personal skills, such as communication or listening skills, are vital if you want to work in a team. Working as a team will mean that each team member will need to communicate with other team members, customers and participants. A brochure giving details of your event must be spelt correctly for example.

● *Technical skills* ●

Technical skills can also be called practical skills – they involve doing things. Some technical skills might include painting, driving or knowing how to operate a particular piece of equipment or sporting apparatus. These are skills that only one person on your team may need to have, such as someone with computer skills to design a poster or leaflet.

▲ **Maintaining gym equipment requires technical skills**

● *Time management skills* ●

Time management is another important skill to look for in team members. Time management means you must work to deadlines – a time or date – by when you must complete your task. If you want to make sure that your event takes place on time then team members need to able to complete jobs on time. Good time management skills also mean that other people with jobs to do are not kept waiting or cannot start their task at all!

CASE STUDY – BRITISH LIONS TOUR

The British Lions rugby team is touring New Zealand in the summer. The tour itinerary is shown below.

Fixture list

DATE	OPPONENT	KICK OFF (GMT)*	KICK OFF (NZT)	VENUE
NEW ZEALAND				
4 June	Bay of Plenty	08:10	19:10	Rotorua International Stadium
8 June	Taranaki	08:10	19:10	Yarrow Stadium, New Plymouth
11 June	NZ Maori	08:10	19:10	Waikato Stadium, Hamilton
15 June	Wellington	08:10	19:10	Westpac Stadium, Wellington
18 June	Otago	08:10	19:10	Carisbrook, Dunedin
21 June	Southland	08:10	19:10	Rugby Park Stadium, Invercargill
25 June	1st Test	08:10	19:10	Jade Stadium, Christchurch
28 June	Manawatu	08:10	19:10	Arena Manawatu, Palmerston North
2 July	2nd Test	08:10	19:10	Westpac Stadium, Wellington
5 July	Auckland	08:10	19:10	Eden Park, Auckland
9 July	3rd Test	08:10	19:10	Eden Park, Auckland

1 Write down three ways in which good time management skills will be important during the tour. Think about travel, meals and training times.

2 The tour takes place in New Zealand. Do you think the 11-hour time difference will affect the players?

3 As the team manager, how would you manage the time to ensure the time difference does not affect the players?

Resources

Resources are all the materials, equipment and specialist helpers that you will need to run an event. This could include the following:

- *specialist staff or officials*
- *equipment needed at the event*
- *money*
- *accommodation for participants, players or officials*
- *training facilities.*

• *Specialist staff and equipment* •

Specialist staff are those with the specialist skills that are essential to your event working. They could be First Aid staff, guides, guest speakers, umpires or coach drivers. Often specialist staff are the people who will operate any equipment that you need, such as speakers, computers, microphones or pool cleaning equipment. You may have to pay these staff to take part in your event, especially if they are professionals, like umpires, catering companies or celebrity guest speakers.

GIVE IT A GO

1 Look at the specialist staff going on the next Lions Rugby Tour by visiting their website – a link is available at www.heinemann.co.uk/hotlinks (express code 0005P).

2 Make a chart of the various staff travelling with the players and write a short description of what their team role is on the tour.

Equipment

For some activities and events, computers and other forms of technology will be required. A sports tournament might need the scores from matches to be recorded on a computer or the times run in a fun run might need to be collected. Posters and programmes can be produced using word processing equipment and then copied on a photocopier to ensure there are sufficient numbers. Obviously, your team would need someone with the necessary skills to use this equipment.

● *Money* ●

When organising your event, it is very important that you identify where money will be spent and on what. Identifying and agreeing costs will make sure that the event does not end up owing money to anyone – this is setting a budget for your event. Setting a budget is working out what the maximum amount of money for a particular part of your event will be and then making sure you do not spend more than that amount. For example, you need to set a budget to pay the specialist staff or for the participants' travel expenses.

The team member responsible for this will need to keep a detailed record of what money has been spent and why. They should also make sure that they keep the receipts as records. At the end of the event, the amount of money allocated and the amount spent should be the same.

Another task involving money might be to find a source of funds, perhaps a sponsor, who will provide the money you need.

EVITENCE ACTIVITY  P2

Skills and resources

In groups, choose one of the three activities below and list and describe all the skills and resources you think would be needed to make each event a success. Be ready to share your work with the rest of the class.

- a sports event
- a car boot sale
- a school fête.

GLOSSARY

Considerations are the things you must take into account or consider.

Contingencies are what you will do if things do not go as planned. For example, if it rains when you are supposed to have a barbecue on the beach, you may move the event indoors as a contingency.

Planning your event

Good planning will be very important to the success of your event. Remember: 'If you fail to plan, you plan to fail.' When planning your event there are four main stages to go through:

- ▻ *the nature and purpose of your event*
- ▻ *the resources you need to make your event a success*
- ▻ ***considerations** and **contingencies***
- ▻ *roles and responsibilities of all those team members involved.*

GIVE IT A GO: why plan?

Look at the following picture of a marathon.

1 Where have all these people parked their cars?

2 What if anyone gets injured?

3 How will you collect results?

4 How important do you think planning is for an event of this size?

The nature and purpose of your event

The first step in planning an event is deciding what type of event you are going to organise and why? Are you planning a five-a-side football competition to find the best team in your centre, or are you trying to raise money for a charity? It is important that, as a team, you are all agreed on what type of event you are going to organise (the nature of the event) and why (the purpose of the event).

Who is the event for? The age range of your intended customers will affect a number of things, for example, young children will need different size footballs to adults. How many participants or spectators are you expecting? This will affect a number of issues such as the amount of space needed, the number of pieces of equipment and refreshments etc. All of these things need to be planned early as they will have an effect on the planning of the rest of the event.

Resources

As you have seen on pages 158–159, your event may need a variety of resources in order to be successful, including:

- *a venue*
- *money*
- *staff*
- *equipment*
- *information.*

Exactly what you need will depend on the type of event to be organised, the reason for organising it and the **client group**. Making a list of what resources you will need, budgeting enough money for each resource and where you will find each resource is a vital part of the planning process.

> ### GLOSSARY
> **Client group** is a term given to all the customers who use a facility or service.

Considerations and contingencies

When organising an event, it is important to consider all the factors that could have an impact on your event. You will need to have a plan for how to deal with each one. Some of the factors to think about include:

- *the weather – what will happen to your car boot sale if it is raining?*
- *safety – how can you make sure all the people standing next to the river during your kayak event are safe?*
- *permission – do you need special permissions to play music, serve alcohol, collect money in the town centre or organise a raffle? Who do you need to get permission from?*
- *arrival and departure – how will people enter and leave your event safely by foot or by car?*

▲ **Outdoor events will need contingency plans for bad weather**

Remember to always think about the purpose of your event and how it will affect your planning. For example, for an event that aims to raise money for a charity you will need to make sure that all the money raised during the event is given to the charity. Any money needed to organise the event should be given by sponsors.

GIVE IT A GO: considerations and contingencies

Look at the following questions and, in small groups, think of some answers. Discuss your answers with the rest of the class.

- Why do school fêtes often take place in the summer?
- What difference will it make to hold a firework show at 6pm in summer, or winter?
- What permissions would be needed to run a marathon around your local town streets?
- Is it more difficult to organise an outdoor event during the winter months? Why?
- What is a duty of care?

No matter how well you plan your event, not everything is in your or your team's control. You will need to make contingencies or have a 'plan B' to make sure that you can cope with any change to your plans. For example, what will you do if the venue you have organised is double booked? Where can you get equipment at the last minute if yours breaks?

...someone gets injured during your sport event?

In groups, discuss how you would cope as a team to:

a prevent an injury

b deal with an injury during an event.

Log onto the St. John Ambulance website for some First Aid tips that may help you – a link is available at www.heinemann.co.uk/hotlinks (express code 0005P).

Roles and responsibilities

All staff involved in your event will need to have an agreed role in the planning, running and evaluation of your chosen event. It is important that this role is clear and that everyone fully understands what they need to do.

• *What is a role?* •

A role is what a person is expected to do. Make sure that everyone is clear about what they are expected to do. Agree these roles and write them down so there can be no argument later.

Some of the roles your team might need include:

- *treasurer – deals with budget and money issues*
- *secretary – keeps minutes of all meetings and looks after other documents*
- *transport – organises transport*
- *venue organiser – finds, chooses and books the venue*
- *fixtures – organising the timing of each match and who plays against whom.*

Every event will need to have people performing different roles. The roles are based on the nature of the event being organised. For example, a fashion show will not need someone to organise fixtures but will need someone to organise rooms for people to change in. Remember to allocate the roles to suit each person's skills, abilities and interests. The best way of making sure that a job gets done well is to make sure that people enjoy their roles. Your team members should want to take on the roles being offered. As a group you need to sit down and agree on what roles are needed and who is going to take them on.

▲ Sit down and agree on everyone's roles

• *What is a responsibility?* •

A responsibility is something that you would be accountable for – it is your duty to make sure it happens. For example, everyone involved in your event will be responsible for the health and safety of all participants, clients and guests during the event. If someone has an accident, then you will all be responsible for any injuries. This could be a very serious matter. All team members must take their roles and responsibilities seriously. This will ensure that there are no accidents and that everyone enjoys themselves in a safe environment.

EVIDENCE ACTIVITY

Plan a sport or leisure event

1 As a team, you have been asked to organise a cross-country event for local schools. There are seven schools entered, each with both a boys' and girls' team. There are six runners in each team.

   a Write a plan for this event by copying and completing the following table. Draw up your findings on a large poster and display it for the rest of the class to see. **P3**

Considerations	What is needed?
Course	
Facilities	
Staff	
Money	
Health and safety	
Accommodation required	
Equipment	
What specialist staff roles are needed?	
Contingencies	
Are there any other considerations?	

2 In pairs, choose one of the following sport or leisure events:

- • kayak endurance race
- • saturday morning ramble
- • school orienteering competition
- • mountain bike race
- • pensioners' bridge tournament.

Using your chosen event write a plan that will ensure that the event will be a success. Remember to think about the nature and purpose of the event, the skills and resources you will need, what roles and responsibilities your team will have, the budget and any contingencies you will need to make.

Organisation and delivery

After all you and your team's planning, now you have to actually do the work to make your event happen! Successful planning will need regular meetings when all those involved get together to discuss any items concerning your event. In your first meeting you should draw up a plan or timetable of when tasks need to be completed or delivered.

GIVE IT A GO: a written plan

In small groups, discuss the advantages of having a written plan for your event. Write down five reasons and then compare your answers with the rest of the class.

Organise

As you can see organising an event is not easy. It requires team work, planning and a range of skills and resources. These must all be pulled together at the same time and place to ensure your event runs successfully. Regular meetings to discuss progress and any problems will help make sure that on the day the event runs smoothly, that everyone involved enjoys themself and that the event meets its aims.

Try to remember:

- ▭ *it is important that you all work together, to help each other*
- ▭ *make sure you agree about what you are organising and why*
- ▭ *make sure that everyone understands his or her roles and responsibilities within the team and that everyone has a role that they want and enjoy*
- ▭ *lots of planning means your event is sure to be a success!*

• *Meetings, agendas, minutes and feedback* •

When holding a meeting, it is important that an agenda is set, minutes are made and that everyone has the chance to give some feedback to the rest of the team.

Agendas

An agenda is a plan of what is to be talked about during the meeting. The following is a sample agenda. You can use it as a template when you write up your own agendas.

Agenda

1.   **OPENING** *Chairperson brings meeting to order and opens with a welcome. She can ask a member to prepare a 'thought for the day' to set the tone of the meeting.*

2.   **ROLL CALL** *Secretary keeps a record of: a. Those present b. Those absent without notification c. Those who sent regrets.*

3.   **MINUTES OF LAST MEETING** *'Are there any errors or omissions?' Errors are corrected, omissions are inserted. Minutes are then declared 'Approved as printed' or 'Approved as corrected'.*

4.   **FINANCIAL STATEMENT** *(If applicable to your committee)*

5.   **BUSINESS ARISING FROM MINUTES** *This item will deal with ongoing business and gives continuity to the work of the committee. Under this heading is listed those matters to be discussed.*

6.   **REPORT OF STAFF PERSON RELATED TO YOUR COMMITTEE**

7.   **REPORTS OF MEMBERS WITH SPECIAL TASK ASSIGNMENTS**

8.   **VISITOR OR SPEAKER** *– if any*

9.   **NEW BUSINESS** *List here those matters which are to be discussed for the first time.*

10.   **CORRESPONDENCE** *– if any*

11.   **DATE OF NEXT MEETING**

12.   **ANNOUNCEMENTS OR MEMOS** *(coming events)*

13.   **ADJOURNMENT** *Chairperson asks, 'Is there any further business to come before the meeting at this time?' Chairperson declares the meeting adjourned.*

▲ A sample agenda

GLOSSARY

Adjourn means to stop a meeting with the intention of continuing at a later date.

Minutes

At the end of the meeting, someone must write up all the points, ideas and notes made during the meeting. These notes are known as the minutes of the meeting. This is a written record of what was said or agreed upon at the meeting. Having written minutes also means that there can be no arguments about what was agreed upon and who is responsible for a particular job. They can also serve as a reminder for people and can be given to team members who were unable to come to the meeting.

Feedback

Meetings allow everyone to have their say and for the team to discuss their event and any issues connected with it. Prior to the day of your event, it is a good idea to have a 'dry run' wherever possible to check that there are no last minute problems or hitches!

Delivering your event

On the day of your event, all the hard work you have all put in will be put to the test. Each team member should have a role for the actual day which tells them what they are expected to do and when – welcome competitors, greet guests, collect the clothes or serve refreshments. It is important that all the team try to keep smiling – this can be a big help, especially if the weather is poor or things are not going to plan!

• *Problem solving* •

It is likely that there will be some problems. Equipment might fail, people might argue with a referee's decision or a child might get lost. It is important that, as a team, you have the ability to solve these problems quickly and efficiently. Being able to do this will keep your event running smoothly and safely and will ensure that customers enjoy themselves.

GIVE IT A GO: solving problems

Consider the following typical last minute problems. Work in small groups and suggest solutions to each one.

Problem	Possible Solution
a piece of important equipment fails	
a team that has entered your tournament does not turn up	
a child becomes separated from his or her parents	
a customer hurts him or herself in a fall	
the weather for a school fête is very wet and windy	
there is a major accident on the road and the coach taking you on a trip is going to be delayed by 1 hour	

Reviewing your event

At the end of your event there will still be jobs to do. Equipment will need to be dismantled and put away or returned, results will need to be sent to all participants, thank-you letters will need to be written to sponsors or guest speakers and the venue will need to be cleaned up.

In addition, your team will need to hold one last meeting to discuss how the event went. This is the review meeting. At this meeting you will ask questions like:

- *Was the event a success? If not, why not?*
- *Did the event achieve its aims?*
- *Were there any problems?*
- *How can these problems be solved so that they do not happen again?*

You should try to get the opinions of the people who took part or attended – competitors, staff who observed your event, guests etc. All of these people can give you vital information to help you **evaluate** your event. Remember, not everything will have gone well. The important thing is to find out why problems occurred. Was it an accident that could not be avoided or was it due to an error by a team member? Some factors will be outside your control – the weather for example. Others, like having the right amount of equipment, are within your control. Collecting feedback and evaluating your event will ensure that you can get it right the next time. Remember that your review meeting is also a chance to congratulate yourselves on a job well done!

▲ **Your review meeting is also a chance to congratulate yourselves on a job well done**

EVIDENCE ACTIVITY

For this task, you will be required to keep a diary which records everything you do in relation to the event to be held. Your diary should include details of: **P4**

- the planned event
- who is involved and each person's role(s)
- dates and times of when and what you did for the event
- records of all meetings you attend and what those meetings agreed.

1 When you complete tasks for the event, make sure a teacher or lecturer signs to confirm these tasks were completed by you.

2 Where possible, if you speak with teachers, lecturers or any other person about the event you are helping to organise, **make sure** they provide a written statement saying what you did, when and so on. Can you produce any other evidence? Photos, witness statements, etc?

3 Record what you actually do **on the day**. Again, obtain as many **different** sources of evidence as you can from other people. In your diary, talk about what went well and **give reasons** why it did so. What contribution did **you** have to the success of the event? Remember, you must make sure that the event would not have been successful without **your** involvement. **M2**

4 At the end of the event, **evaluate** the success of the event. Give reasons why things did or did not go well. Remember, some may have been out of your control (e.g. the weather), while others will have been under your control (e.g. the amount of food and drink ordered or the number of seats provided for spectators). Imagine you have been asked to do the same event again next month – what would you change or do differently and why? **D1**

Find the answers to the questions in the puzzle. They could be written across, down or diagonally, backwards or forwards.

```
A Q W F P S E R B U D G E T W M E M M S E S T A
R C T F L Y O U R U C I Q F J E V O F T P O C G
W O R M L L D U T Y O F C A R E Z O F R V O Z E
I M O N F H O B R X N V T I T M E S Y I P L A N
S M K S K F O W O R V A L R K M P T H A S E S D
T U E B T C H A I R P E R S O N L Y F E V U A A
I N J S U V P L S E O F R N C I V G F D C O N F
K I O D P I R S T L V U G E D N A E A I R O O G
Z C H O T M C O N H J I R H S G L F M G M M G J
C A X J W O R K I N G W I T H O T H E R S E X A
A T S G E S M E B H S S B W O R U O D C V F S R
R E V A L U A T E D D T A S F U Y R X C O I E S
B L R X Z I N G K O W S M T W F Q B C U O M R T
O D P M L W G E V M O A E M G J Z U C E V T L A
O T E M F F F N E L B U D R O U R D U Y S I A F
T L R Y S T M S N L C O N T I N G E N C Y B N F
S A Q A I R W T U L P M E S T O H Q W O R B S G
A V C U S T O M E R S E R V I C E V P N D E I N
L P I G Q Z R J P N C O M R U O C P L V K D V X
E A L E U F O O P K R E S W F F L I C E N C E O
```

1 Team members need to be able to _____ with each other and with customers.

2 ____ are equipment and people you need to organise an event.

3 Team members need to use the key skill _____.

4 Having a _____ will ensure that people enjoy themselves and the event runs smoothly.

5 Your event will need a _____ to make sure you do not overspend.

6 You have a _____ to keep your customers safe.

7 The _____ is where the event takes place.

8 You will need good _____ skills in order to deal with people attending the event.

9 A meeting needs to have an _____ to ensure everything is discussed.

10 After your event it will need to be _____.

11 Your event committee will need a _____ to run the meetings.

12 If your event is outdoors, you will need a _____ for bad weather.

13 You will need lots of _____ to help you run the event.

14 If you will have live music at your event you will need a _____.

15 A _____ is an event where people sell unwanted goods.

unit 8

Issues in sport and leisure

In this unit you will learn about the relationship between sport and leisure activities and different groups of people. You will also look at the rules, regulations, issues and practices that try to make sure all people are able to enjoy and take part in sport and leisure. Sport and leisure has a big part to play in our social lives and for some it is a way of earning a living or even doing business. We all have different reasons why we take part in sport and leisure activities: for health and fitness, fun or achievement. Different groups of people prefer different activities and have varying needs, which can lead to different issues and practices.

This unit will help lay the foundations of how to apply proper **standards** in sport and leisure settings. It will explore experiences of **current practitioners** and **role models** and ask you to look at your own experiences. You will be able to look at one area in more depth and present information on a specific sport or activity.

This unit is internally assessed. This means, to pass this unit, you will complete an assignment set and marked by your tutor.

> ### GLOSSARY
>
> **Standards** are levels of behaviour and personal values that are set for people to achieve at work, for example being fair all the time.
> **Current practitioners** are people who are working in the sports industry.
> **Role models** are people who young people admire and want to be like.

In this unit you will need to learn about:

- ▷ the relationships between sport and leisure and different groups of people
- ▷ the influences in sport and leisure
- ▷ good practice in delivery of sport and leisure activities
- ▷ different issues in sport and leisure.

Groups of people

People who work in sport and leisure need to have a good awareness of the groups of people they will work with and the range of activities these people prefer. As a coach or activity leader you will have to respect people's needs and individuality. Sport and leisure centre managers or activity planners will usually look at the groups of people who use the centre regularly to help them plan programmes and activities – this is called **segmentation**.

Groups of people can be grouped according to a number of factors:

▲ People can be grouped according to a number of factors

● *Age groups* ●

Segmenting people into age groups is the easiest and most common way of grouping people. People of different ages will enjoy different leisure and sport activities. In the sport and leisure industry, activity programmes and events are often targeted at specific age groups.

Age group	Activities
Children	Fun activities, especially at holiday times, such as short tennis, mini-rugby, crafts or potted sports
Teenagers	More structured events such as football training or regular club nights
Young adults	Competitions and skills development such as martial arts or basketball
Adults	Regular leagues or clubs
The elderly	Low impact activities with a social element such as badminton, bingo, cards or bowls

• *Locations and nationalities* •

People can also be grouped according to where they come from or their nationalities. As a sport or leisure planner, knowing what sport and leisure interests people from different countries or locations have is important because it could affect which activities will be popular at your centre. For example, most Australians will play rugby league, whereas in the UK the more popular form of the game is rugby union. Each game has different rules and is played with a different sized ball. If you were organising a rugby game between a touring Australian rugby club and your local rugby club, you would need to make sure everyone knew which form of the game was to be played!

• *Abilities and disabilities* •

All people have different levels of ability. It is important to offer activities that will appeal to people of all abilities. This can mean offering different classes for a particular activity, such as yoga, to groups of beginners, improvers or advanced participants. Imagine how frustrating and possibly dangerous it could be to have a first-time yoga student trying an advanced yoga position such as a headstand.

▲ **Don't mix beginners with advanced students!**

Another group of people who have specific leisure and sport needs, are those with disabilities. Many more people are becoming aware of the special needs of people with disabilities. Sport and leisure facilities must now be able to offer access to everyone, for example, Ripon Leisure Centre Wheelchair Football Group and the Sussex Wasps Sports Disability Group. Events such as the Paralympics help raise awareness and give an opportunity to improve the facilities and provision of sport and leisure activities for able and disabled athletes.

• *Race, religion and gender* •

People are often grouped according to their race, religion or gender. This is a very sensitive way of grouping people as it can lead to discrimination. You must never discriminate against people, especially based on their race, religion or gender. It can be useful, however, to be aware of people's cultural backgrounds if you want to plan successful, accessible and popular sport and leisure events. For example, if your sport or leisure centre is in an area where many immigrants from Africa live, you may think about organising an Africa Week with drumming and dance workshops, or a gospel choir event. Some religions do not allow men and women to play sport together; some sport and leisure clubs offer a women-only session to ensure that everyone has a chance to use their facilities in a comfortable environment.

• *Socio-economic groups* •

Dividing people into socio-economic groups is a way of grouping people according to what they earn. Many people are unable to take part in sport and leisure activities because they cannot afford the membership or entrance fees or the personal equipment, such as trainers or swimming costumes. Understanding the socio-economic grouping of the people who use your sport and leisure centre can be useful when you are planning how much to charge for activities, whether you need to provide equipment, transport, refreshments or if you need to organise sponsorship for an event.

Many local authority sport centres and voluntary groups work hard to provide all groups with opportunities to take part in sport and leisure activities. This may mean offering free taster sessions, free equipment or low-cost coaching. There are also sports development schemes that are designed to give everyone a chance to play sport and be active. Many of these schemes are dependent on funding from the UK government or European Union (EU) or use lottery-funded facilities to kick-start participation.

CASE STUDY – CARDIFF'S SPORT DEVELOPMENT TEAM

Cardiff has a sport development team which aims to increase leisure participation at **grass-roots** level and to provide opportunities for all the people in Cardiff to take part in sport. They work closely with schools to improve the amount and quality of after-school sport and leisure opportunities for children and to link them with the greater community.

The sports development team consists of:

- one manager or team leader
- five sport-specific development officers in football, rugby league, tennis, rugby union and cricket

- two general sport development officers, covering a range of sports from netball to squash
- one person who works with people with learning disabilities.

1 What do you think of the size of this development team?

2 Log onto the Cardiff Sport Development Team website – a link is available at www.heinemann.co.uk/hotlinks (express code 0005P). What else is the sports development team doing to encourage people to take part in sport?

GLOSSARY

Grass roots is a term used to describe the lower levels of sport where talent is grown, for example local clubs.

175

● *Challenges for sport and leisure organisers* ●

The issue for sport leaders or leisure activity organisers is to choose the right combination of sport or leisure activities to meet the needs of as many people as possible. This can be done by talking to the people who use the centre to find out why they use the centre, what they do like and don't like and what other activities they would like to see at the centre. It might also be useful to ask non-users to see why they don't come to the centre. Some reasons may be the price, opening and closing times are inconvenient or they don't have the skills (they can't swim or don't know the rules of bridge).

The main challenge for programmers in sport and leisure centres is allocating time and space to each user group. Managers cannot discriminate against any one group.

EVIDENCE ACTIVITY

Different age groups

1 Choose four age groups and list different sport and leisure activities that each group might enjoy.

2 Explain why some people would take part in each sport or activity and not others.

Activities

In the previous section you looked at a number of examples of sports and leisure activities that different people enjoy. Certain groups and types of individuals prefer certain activities. Looking at what groups people belong to and the activities that they enjoy also helps sport and leisure planners decide which facilities and events will be popular in certain areas. Below are some ideas that have been used in the past for varying groups and their sporting needs:

- *cricket grounds were mostly built by rich Victorians for public schoolboys to play on*
- *aerobics gave young women a way into health and fitness*
- *badminton or bowls really suit older players as they are less active activities*
- *jogging is one of the leading activities for both men and women*
- *swimming is one of the most popular activities for all ages.*

▲ **Mixed-team basketball is popular with young adults**

GIVE IT A GO: popular sport activities

1 What is the most popular national sport? What is the most popular leisure activity? Give reasons for your answers.

2 What is the most popular activity in your area? Why do you think that it is the most popular?

Below are some ideas of leisure activities which have become more popular in the last decade:

- *bingo has improved its prizes and made a come back as a popular day- and night-time activity, with women in particular*
- *shopping has become a hobby for some people and huge malls have been built to support this need, for example Meadowhall, Metrocentre, Bluewater and the Trafford Centre*
- *home-based leisure has seen the biggest boom with electronic toys and games targeted at young people*
- *home-based entertainment systems for adults – plasma screens and digital TV home cinemas*
- *home-based do-it-yourself – there are many popular TV programmes that look at how to improve your home and garden.*

▲ Many people spend their leisure time in shopping malls

For each of the activities listed on page 177, which groups of people do you think they appeal to? Think about age, gender and socio-economic groups of people. Be ready to share your answers with the rest of the class.

Relationships

GLOSSARY

Provision means making available and accessible.

In the last section you learnt about some of the relationships between sports, **provision**, leisure activities and different groups of people. The way groups of people interact and the types of activities they choose often change – as they change so will their needs. If you are planning activities at a centre then you will need to make sure that your centre develops and changes to reflect those needs.

• *Needs* •

People's needs are complex and can depend on many factors, such as their socio-economic status, their motivations or social and sporting needs. For example, some people come to the leisure centre to meet friends, while others come to get fit and some people come to do both! The government is encouraging sport and leisure organisations to try and widen participation so that all types of need can be met.

• *Resources* •

Being able to meet varying needs also depends on the resources of a sport and leisure centre. Resources are things like sports buildings or halls, finance for leisure developments and staff to run the facilities. These are nearly always limited and often have to serve a social as well as sporting need. For example, children in the UK are encouraged to do 30 minutes of exercise a day to try to decrease the number of cases of obesity in children. To meet this need there needs to be access to more (and cheaper) sport facilities.

• *Developments and changes* •

Many sport and leisure developments reflect the changes in the way that people enjoy their sport and leisure time. Some recent examples include, multi-activity centres, for example Xscapes in Milton Keynes and Castleford, where you can shop, see a film or even spend an hour snowboarding! As more people take part in sport and leisure activities, there has been an increase in the demand for leisure activities and facilities, such as private gyms and clubs.

▲ Shop, watch a film and even snowboard – all under one roof!

● *Barriers* ●

Despite the increase in the need for sport and leisure activities, there are still a number of people who do not have access to sport and leisure facilities because of barriers. Barriers can range from lack of money or abilities, cultural issues, location, confidence, disability or attitudes and can be an issue for many types of people.

Certain groups in society find it more difficult than others to participate in sport or leisure activities. The kinds of difficulties they face include:

- *some religions prevent women from playing sport in the same areas as men*
- *lack of knowledge of UK sports in places where only UK-based sport activities are offered*
- *people on low incomes or the unemployed who cannot afford equipment, membership or entry fees*
- *inability to speak English*
- *location – groups of people in the countryside will not be able to access the same range of facilities as those in towns or cities*
- ***ability*** *– they may lack skill, motivation or education, all of which are parts of ability.*

> **GLOSSARY**
>
> **Ability** refers to how well you can do something.

GIVE IT A GO: barriers to sport and leisure

1 Add three more barriers that you know of to the list.
2 Go to your local sport or leisure centre and look for examples of how they are trying to ensure all people are able to participate. For example, do they have disabled access, signs in different languages or offer different types of classes or activities?

● *How does it all fit together?* ●

Providing sport and leisure activities to as many people as possible depends on a range of issues. All these issues interact and today sport and leisure centres have to meet a range of needs. For example:

- *needs are different for each group of people*
- *resources can only be found if there are sporting and social benefits*
- *developments need funding from sponsors and government initiatives to get them started*
- *barriers to participation are a big issue for the **governing bodies of sport** which want more people and more achievement*

The **funding stream** of the national lottery has given a lot of money to help stimulate and support these integrated relationships and overcome barriers.

> **GLOSSARY**
>
> **Governing bodies of sport** are organisations set up to manage sport, for example the FA or the Volleyball Association. **Funding streams** are sources or flows of money.

... *we did not use lottery money for sports funding?*

In pairs, think of at least three other ways that sport could be funded. For example, would you pay a 1 percent sports tax instead?

CASE STUDY – THE HILLSBOROUGH ARENA

The Hillsborough Arena is built on the site of the City of Sheffield's old athletics stadium and is very close to the home of Sheffield Wednesday FC. The Arena's club-house building is the focal point of the site. Inside is the members' bar, a multi-purpose indoor hall, a meeting room and five heated changing rooms with showers. There are a number of classes and sessions held in the hall during the week, including fitness workouts, table tennis matches and karate. The sprung floor and high ceiling make it ideal for table tennis.

The clubhouse, along with the all-weather pitches, was built with money from Sport England's lottery fund. Until its opening in 1998, those using the Arena had to use old facilities housed in the old running track's original buildings, they now have a super facility for the community.

1 Do you think that lottery money should be spent on sports improvements in the UK?

2 What other sources of funding are available to help schemes like the Hillsborough Arena?

Influences

We are all exposed every day to communications designed to influence our attitudes and spending through a range of mediums – magazines, TV, mobile phones and the radio. The message they send out may be to look healthier or wear different clothes, but the underlying message is to buy more products!

Role models

Even sporting and celebrity role models influence our attitudes and spending, as they promote and endorse products as part of deals that add to their incomes. The media often reports on negative role models such as sport or celebrity personalities involved with drugs, violence, cheating and corruption.

There are still some sporting role models who have set themselves high standards, for example, Sir Steve Redgrave, Tanni Grey Thompson and Ellen MacArthur. Able and disabled athletes can model themselves on these influences and can be inspired by them.

The media

Maybe one of the biggest issues in sport today is its relationship with the media. Some people say that professional sport cannot exist without media involvement because it brings in a lot of money and sponsorships. Some sports have enjoyed a huge revival due to the TV coverage they get, such as snooker and bowls. Coverage of sport events provides entertainment on the radio, in magazines, on the Internet and through other electronic or print media. These are some of the positive issues in the relationship between sport and the media.

The main negative issue is advertising. Advertising has a great influence on leisure habits as well influencing fashion, music and entertainment. People who cannot afford to spend money on non-essential products can often feel left out or disadvantaged.

Initiatives and policy

Policies or plans are usually made at the highest level in an organisation and then passed down for others to take action. Some sports policies are made at the government level by the Department for Culture, Media and Sport (DCMS) and passed on to sports organisations such as Sport England or the FA. The organisations that must apply these policies usually create their own initiatives to achieve the desired aims. The policies of more inclusion through sport and more sport in school to reduce obesity, for example, led to an FA initiative called Football in the Community.

EVIDENCE ACTIVITY P2

The influence of the media

Create a scrapbook of pictures, articles, advertising and reports that show both positive and negative influences of the media in sport and leisure. Look in newspapers, magazines, advertising brochures or leaflets and on the Internet.

Good practice

Good practice is a term used to describe the best way of doing things. Through research and experience leading bodies in the sport and leisure industry, such as Skills Active, SportscoachUK and Sport England (links to these site are available at www.heinemann.co.uk/hotlinks, express code 0005P), set standards of good or best practice which they share with other people and facilities around the country.

Good practice can also be called ethical practices – ways of doing things that ensure fairness and equality. The EU has a sports charter which lays out many of the principles to follow. The following are some of the basic ideas expressed in the EU Charter for Sport.

- *The Sport Movement* – local governments are expected to be at the heart of the work done.
- *Facilities and activities* – access to facilities and activities for all is a basic right.
- *Building the foundation* – sport among young people and children should be encouraged.
- *Developing participation* – participation should be developed for all types of leisure.
- *Improving performance* – playing sport at professional levels and talent spotting should be encouraged and supported with coaching and sports science.
- *Top level and professional sport* – encouraging people to play sport professionally should be supported with top-level facilities and programmes.

THINK ABOUT IT

As a class, discuss what you think the main themes of the EU Charter for Sport are. How do you think this charter affects sport and leisure providers in the UK?

Areas of good practice

Good and ethical practices are necessary in a number of areas to ensure fairness and equality. Let's look at some examples of this: equity, use of resources, respecting rights, needs and targets.

• *Equity* •

Equity at work means treating everybody equally, whether they are male, female, young, old, rich, poor, able or disabled.

All areas of work should show **equitable good practice**. For example, in coaching, a sport coach must:

- *use a caring approach*
- *identify each individual player's needs*
- *make an equal commitment regardless of ability*
- *protect young players from bad practice, such as cheating*
- *build trust and respect with players.*

GLOSSARY

Equitable good practices are fair and honest ways of working.

CASE STUDY – PROVIDING EQUAL OPPORTUNITIES

North Kesteven Sports Outreach Team from Lincolnshire helps develop sport within communities. They encourage disabled people to participate in sport by increasing access to facilities and breaking down the barriers that are commonly met by disabled participants. The team does this by offering disabled people the chance to take part in sporting activities within the community and also by giving advice to existing sports clubs on how to welcome disabled athletes.

The team is responsible for planning and organising many of the district council's successful annual events. These include the 'On your marks' holiday scheme, which sends qualified sports coaches to villages through-out the district, giving children the chance to take part in a structured sporting activity. The team works closely with schools in the area to find teams for the annual Lincolnshire Youth Games, and plans to increase the disabled athlete's events for this.

1 Make a list of all the disability-friendly clubs or facilities in your area.

2 Do you think able-bodied people should participate in sport and leisure activities for people with disabilities? Why?

● *Use of resources* ●

Using resources equitably means that you and your organisation use your resources in a way that makes sure as many people benefit as possible. This also means using resources for the best possible result. For example, using resources equitably means trying to make equipment last as long as possible, buying better quality to last longer, not having large amounts of wastage and repairing where possible before replacing.

GLOSSARY

Human rights are the rights we have as individuals, for example freedom of speech and the right to fair treatment.

● *Respecting rights* ●

We all have basic **human rights** and it is just as important to maintain them in the sport and leisure industry as anywhere else.

Children's rights

For sport and leisure activities that involve children you need to be aware of children's rights. Young children have the right to be protected from adults who may influence them in bad practice, for example taking drugs or abusing them.

Anyone who is going to be working closely with children must have a police check to make sure they do not have a past record of mistreating children.

GIVE IT A GO: child protection

The Children Act (1989) is the law that states what rights children have.

1 Look this act up in the library or on the Internet.

2 Write down five ways in which this act could affect your work in the sport and leisure industry.

Data protection

Another area where the rights of people using sport and leisure facilities are protected is data protection. This affects places that hold personal information in databases, either in a paper file or electronically. For example, a sport centre may have a record of its members' addresses or payment details. The Data Protection Act protects people from having their personal information given out to the general public. (See Unit 5, pages 122–123 for more information on the Data Protection Act, 1998.)

WHAT if?

... the government did not insist on data protection?

1 Log onto the Data Protection Act website – a link is available at www.heinemann.co.uk/hotlinks (express code 0005P) and look at what the Data Protection Act (1998) means.

2 What might happen if we could not find out who held information on us?

● *Needs* ●

As you have already learnt in this unit, different groups of people have different needs. Sport and leisure centres try to meet as many of their customers' needs as possible (read Unit 10, pages 222–223 for more information on customer needs).

Often groups of people with special needs, such as disabled athletes or members of some religious groups, find that their needs are not met. They may be discriminated against by providers that do not offer sports or activities they can take part in.

Sometimes action is needed to make sure that this does not happen: this is called **positive discrimination**. Some examples of positive discrimination are:

▭ *adapted games*
▭ *times and facilities suited to special-needs participants*
▭ *extra training for staff*
▭ *sports development schemes.*

GLOSSARY

Positive discrimination is a way of helping people who are disadvantaged, for example adding access for disabled athletes to sports venues.

185

• *Targets* •

Many sports governing bodies and local authority leisure providers set themselves good practice targets. This is a way of ensuring that their organisations show good practice, fairness and 'sport opportunities for all'. These targets can be measured after a period of time or after a programme or event has been run. The following are examples of the kinds of good practice targets that a sport and leisure organisation could set:

▷ *encouraging 20 more people to take part in exercise classes*
▷ *to run a one-day taster in sports for people over 50*
▷ *to have an open day*
▷ *run a five-a-side football tournament for disadvantaged youth.*

Many targets are set for different organisations across the country because a lot of the same problems can be found nationally.

CASE STUDY – SCOTTISH SPORT INCLUSION PROGRAMME

In Scotland, as part of a new sport inclusion programme, seven projects were given a total of £353,240 in 2002. Each of the projects taking part in the programme had to raise 10 percent of the costs themselves. Each of the projects were from disadvantaged areas. Six of the projects are outlined below.

- Paisley Partnership Regeneration Company: Health improvement through sport (HITS) – £115,348

- South Coatbridge SIP: Parent action for safe play – £22,574

- Eastbank Health Promotion Centre: Dance activity group – £11,576

- South Edinburgh SIP: Sports and recreation activity programme – £51,585

- Forres Skate/BMX Club, Moray Youth Start: construction of BMX/skateboarding equipment – £5,743

- Dundee City Council, SIP 1 and 2: Youth sport development project – £133,789.

1 Which age group is targeted by these schemes?

2 Why do you think these projects have chosen to run programmes for this age group?

3 In small groups think of two other programmes that a sport or leisure organisation could run that would benefit this age group.

4 Choose another group of people. In your small groups, plan two activities that your chosen groups would benefit from.

Standards

Standards and good practice are very similar. Standards are the rules of good practice. In the late 1990s the leading skills organisation for sport and leisure, SPRITO (now called Skills Active) (a link is available at www.heinemann.co.uk/hotlinks, express code 0005P) sent out a document on the best practice rules for coaches, teachers and leaders in the sport and leisure industry.

These rules or standards were created for several areas of work in the sport and leisure industry, such as:

- *outdoor education, development, training and recreation*
- *sport development*
- *staff working in recreational facilities*
- *playwork*
- *coaching, teaching and instructing.*

In each of these work areas, rules were set for professional standards, relationships and the responsibilities of sport and leisure workers. We will look at the coaching, teaching and instructing work area as an example of what standards are used for and how important they are to the sport and leisure industry.

▲ **The instructor is on the water first, giving instruction. Can you spot any problems?**

WHAT if?

... coaches were not controlled by rules and standards?

In small groups discuss why you think it is important to set rules and standards for coaches, sport and leisure planners and leaders.

• *Professional standards* •

Professional standards are the rules that all professional sport and leisure workers must obey. These standards look at the way you work with other people in particular (see below for an example).

> Summary chart of good practice and best values for working in sport and leisure with children:
>
> - make sure that children are at the heart of the activity in a caring, considerate way
> - leaders should guide but not control experiences and behaviour
> - the playing environment needs to be stimulating and help children's self-esteem and confidence to grow
> - children should be treated as individuals with their own rights
> - co-operative socialising effects must be engendered as well as fun.

EVIDENCE ACTIVITY

Personal standards in coaching

Look in magazines and newspapers and on TV and the Internet to help you with the following questions.

1 Look in the recent media to find two examples of good and bad practice of coaches or athletes. Create a poster to show the rest of the class your findings. **(P3)**

2 Describe the examples you found in **1**, to the rest of the class. Explain why they are examples of good and/or bad practice. **(M2)**

3 In pairs, write a report that describes how good and bad practice is influenced by sport and leisure issues, such as the media and advertising. **(D1)**

• *Relationships* •

In all work areas in the sport and leisure industry you will be working with other people. You will build different kinds of relationships with many different people. For example, as a coach you will spend a lot of time guiding and teaching participants and as a salesperson in a sport shop you will have brief meetings with people where you provide a service. No matter what level of relationship you have with the people you come across in your work area, you have to follow standards of good practice.

These relationships need to be based on trust and respect, with concern shown for well-being, safety and **development of independence**. Sports and activity leaders should not show **favouritism** or have excessive or inappropriate physical contact. They are also expected to make sure that young players are treating each other with respect – this means making sure that there is no jealousy, dislike or mistrust within a squad of players.

In their work coaches, teachers and leaders need to think about the players' futures and teach them life skills that they can use in different areas of their lives, such as good behaviour and training or playing habits.

• *Responsibilities* •

In all relationships you have certain responsibilities, also known as your duty of care (see pages 36–37). This is very important if your job is to manage or organise people. You are responsible for the health, safety and welfare of your clients, customers, participants and fellow team members.

Coaching good practice means being responsible for your athletes needs in a number of areas, such as health and safety and use of information – coaches in particular must respect **confidentiality**. Sport officials have a responsibility to be completely **impartial** and stick to the same rules or regulations for every performer. If they see bad behaviour in athletes they have a responsibility to report it and deal with it through the correct standards.

Consequences of being irresponsible

The consequences of breaking standards of good practice or showing bad practice are severe for some coaches, teachers and leaders. You can be asked to leave your job and be banned from coaching again, fined and even sent to prison. The least you could expect would be **blacklisting**, which might mean you could never work as a sport coach or leisure activity leader again.

> **GLOSSARY**
>
> **Development of independence** means helping young players to think and make decisions by themselves. **Favouritism** means treating some people better than others.

> **GLOSSARY**
>
> **Confidentiality** is not releasing private or personal information about someone. **Impartial** means treating everyone equally.

> **GLOSSARY**
>
> **Blacklisting** is being put on a list of people who are not welcome or employable for some reason.

Issues

There are a range of issues in the sport and leisure industry that leisure and sport leaders and participants may face. Some of the issues deal with different groups of people and their needs, access to activities, scarce resources and issues of bad practice and low standards. Governing bodies and government initiatives work hard to overcome these issues and make the sport and leisure industry a fair and equitable area for all. As a sport and leisure worker, being aware of what the issues are will help you to be fair in your work too.

You have already looked at **gender issues**, religious and **cultural barriers**, access and affordability of sports and leisure, in this unit. In this final section you will look at some other issues that fall under two main headings:

▭ *health*
▭ *events*.

Health

Medical research and sports science show that sport and leisure have a big role to play in health and well-being. The government has set up many initiatives, including sport and leisure organisations, to help people stay healthy.

> ### GLOSSARY
>
> **Gender issues** are issues about being male or female, for example sexual orientation.
> **Cultural barriers** are when access to sport can be denied because of a person's cultural, ethnic or religious background.

GIVE IT A GO: health issues

1 Look at the following health issues. With a partner, think of the ways that sport and leisure activities can help deal with these issues:
   • eating disorders
   • heart disease
   • asthma
   • obesity.
2 Look on the Internet to see if you can find any examples of sport and leisure organisations that are running programmes to deal with these issues.

The government is very worried about the increase in the number of cases of obesity in the UK. The UK statistics from the Blood Pressure Association – a link is available at www.heinemann.co.uk/hotlinks (express code 0005P), on obesity show that it is a serious problem.

▭ *Around one in five adults are obese; in 2001 23 percent of women and 21 percent of men were obese.*
▭ *More than half the adult population is overweight.*

◌ *Obesity among 6–15-year-olds has gone from 5 percent in 1990 to 16 percent in 2001.*

◌ *Overweight young people have a 50 percent chance of being overweight adults.*

Lack of sport and active home-based leisure activities, fewer children walking to and from school, a busy school curriculum where time for exercise and sport is cut and poor diet, all add to the number of people becoming obese.

WHAT if?

... you were all made to walk to school?

In groups, discuss the benefits for children of walking to school, college or work.

Events

Sports and leisure events are big business, especially the mega-events like the Olympics and Football World Cup. They bring money to the region holding the event but also the chance to develop many new sport and leisure facilities – this is why London wants to host the 2012 Olympics.

There are a number of issues involved in hosting a **hallmark event**. Manchester recently hosted the Commonwealth games. Some of the issues that Manchester faced are discussed below.

A lot of money is needed just to bid for the event – to pay people's salaries etc. This money is used whether the city wins the bid or not. The issue was deciding who would pay for the bid – public funds, the lottery or private sponsors? There were reports of bad practice in the handling of money, where people paid bribes to the officials who make the final decision.

Building and redevelopment of venues and accommodation were needed, land was bought and designs made up – all expensive resources. The issue was what happens to the facilities after the event?

Closer to the event itself, the opening and closing ceremonies, the running order of all the events and the awards ceremonies were planned. During this stage large numbers of volunteers were used.

During the games there was a lot of pressure on athletes to win and break records. There is always the issue that athletes may be tempted to cheat, adopt 'dirty' tactics or take drugs to get an edge over opponents. This is a very negative issue.

> **GLOSSARY**
>
> **Hallmark events** are major sports events that attract big crowds and media coverage, for example Football World Cup.

While there are a lot of issues to deal with when planning and running a large event, there are some real benefits too:

⮑ *an area benefits from new buildings and sport and leisure venues*
⮑ *a town, city or country puts itself into the international media and is able to promote tourism*
⮑ *some businesses benefit from increased customers.*

WHAT **if?**

... *a town made a real mess of hosting an event?*

With a partner, discuss what the consequences of hosting an unsuccessful event might be.

GIVE IT A GO: London 2012

If London is successful in its bid for the Olympics in 2012, it will be a once-in-a-lifetime opportunity for the borough of Newham. The Games (and Paralympics) are much more than just the greatest sporting spectacular on earth. They promise to deliver real benefits to East London and to Newham in particular:

- thousands of jobs and training opportunities
- new homes
- the biggest park in London
- world-class sports facilities
- thousands of pounds of tourist spending.

1 Can you add two other benefits?

2 Make a list of at least five negative influences hosting the Olympics might have on the people of London.

EVITENCE ACTIVITY

Issues in sport and leisure

1 Working in small groups, create a picture board showing some of the important issues faced in the sport and leisure industry. **P4**

2 Using the picture board you created in **1**, make a presentation to the rest of your class describing what each of the issues is. **M3**

3 Choose one of the issues you described in **2**. Compile a report that looks in detail at this issue. Think about the influences that affect this issue and what standards of good practice are used in the sport and leisure industry to deal with it. **D1**

Find the answers to the questions in the puzzle. They could be written across, down or diagonally, backwards or forwards.

1   The word used to describe how people are split into groups.

2   The disabled athletes world games.

3   Abbreviation for the English Institute of Sport.

4   Popular indoor game, but not a sport.

5   The abbreviated name for the governing body of soccer in England.

6   England's main sporting body.

7   All coaches have to be like this in the way they treat their athletes.

8   The number one guideline for coaches, referees and sports leaders.

9   A word to describe people who are overweight.

10 Top class events are given this name.

unit 9

Taking part in sport

This unit gives you the chance to both learn about different sport activities and to take part in sport yourself. You will look at how sport is organised, learn what fitness is and what factors make up fitness. You will also need to participate in at least one team and one individual sport. This is a very practical unit and much of the evidence you gather to pass this unit will be practical evidence.

This unit is internally assessed. This means, to pass this unit, you will complete an assignment set and marked by your tutor.

In this unit you will need to learn about:

▭ a range of sports
▭ skills, techniques and fitness components related to selected sports
▭ participating in a range of selected sports
▭ reviewing performance.

Range of sports

There are many different sports around the world.

In small groups, collect a sheet of flip chart and a board marker pen. On your flip chart, write down as many different sports as you can think of! Give yourself ten minutes to do this.

How do we classify sports?

Sports can be classified in a number of ways. Sports like football and basketball are team sports. This means there is more than one player on each team, each having a different role but sharing the same overall aim. On the other hand, individual sports involve only one player on each side. Some sports can be both. In tennis, you can play both individually or as a team, when playing doubles. Sports can be classified in a number of different ways. These include:

- *the nature of the game:* *for example, whether the game is played over a net (e.g. tennis, badminton, volleyball) or aiming for a target (e.g. golf, archery, bowls); whether you are able to play in your opponent's space (e.g. football) or whether you must stay in your own space (e.g. volleyball)*
- *the equipment used:* *for example, cricket is a bat and ball game*
- *the place the sport is played:* *for example, swimming is a water sport*
- *what time of the year the sport is played:* *for example, skiing is a winter sport, whereas athletics is a summer sport.*

GIVE IT A GO: classifying sport

In the *Give it a go* activity on page 196, how many different sport activities did you think of? Now look at your list again.

1 Can you see any factors that are common to more than one sport? For example, football, rugby and basketball are all team sports.

2 Complete the following table. An example is done for you.

Description	Category	Example
Sport activities that take place on snow or ice	Winter sport	Skiing
Sport activities where you aim at something		
Sport activities you play with others		
Sport activities where you have no team mates		
Sport activities where you attack an opponent's territory		
Sport activities where you hit a ball or shuttle		
Sport activities, like tennis and squash, are played on these		
Sport activities where you are required to run, throw or jump		
Hockey, football and rugby are played on one of these		
These sport activities would come in a box		
These sport activities require performers to adopt extreme body positions and move over and around various equipment		
These sport activities do not take place on land		

From the table above you can see that there is a huge range of types of sports that take place in different environments and arenas. These are all different classifications of sport.

How is sport organised?

Sport is organised like a pyramid. At the top is a world governing body, for example in football the world governing body is FIFA – the Fédération Internationale de Football Association. Then there are various bodies that organise football in different parts of the world like Asia and Europe, for example, UEFA organises football in Europe, but it follows the rules and regulations set by FIFA. There are then governing bodies for sport in each country – football in the UK is organised by The Football Association (FA). Finally each county has its own governing body looking after football in that specific area of the country. For example, the Cambridgeshire County FA looks after football in Cambridgeshire and it manages all football teams that play in that county.

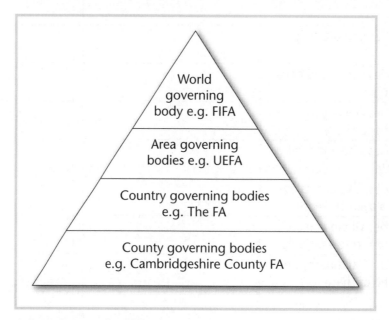

▲ Sport is organised like a pyramid

These organisations ensure that sport is played to a particular standard and according to certain rules and regulations. They manage both professional and **amateur** sport.

• *National governing bodies* •

All sports are organised by a national governing body. These organisations are very important to sport. Without them, sport as we know it would not exist!

Governing bodies carry out a number of important jobs that help to keep their sport fun, safe and interesting.

National governing bodies carry out a number of important roles. These include:

▢ *setting and changing the rules of the game*
▢ *organising competitions*
▢ *promoting the game to all people*
▢ *training coaches and officials*
▢ *funding the game at **grass roots level**.*

▲ **Developing skills at grass roots level**

The best known example of a national governing body is the Football Association (FA). The FA is the national governing body for football in England – a link to their site can be found at www.heinemann.co.uk/hotlinks (express code 0005P).

On the site you will see that the FA carries out many important functions. It:

▢ ***develops** the grass roots, amateur and professional game in England*
▢ ***regulates** the game through rules and laws*
▢ *gives permission, approval and support for all games and competitions played in England*
▢ *organises its own competitions and leagues, such as The FA Cup*
▢ *is in charge of the **disciplinary system** for football in England.*

GLOSSARY

Grass roots level is a term used to describe where beginners learn to play a sport and where people play mainly for enjoyment.

GLOSSARY

Develop means to improve the game in all areas by encouraging more people to play the game or by training a more successful national side.

GLOSSARY

To **regulate** means to control. A governing body of sport regulates (or controls) all aspects of that sport.

GLOSSARY

A **disciplinary system** is a series of steps (or procedures) and punishments that are used to deal with players who break the rules of the sport. Thus in football, players who receive a red card receive an automatic ban from the sport for a certain length of time. More serious cases might involve a fine or punishment.

The FA has worked very hard to encourage more and more people to take part in football – as both players and spectators of the game. As a result, football is very successful and the game has more spectators, participants, money coming in and media coverage than ever before.

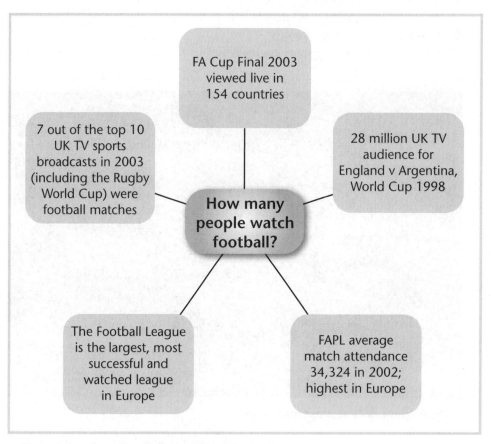

▲ Some facts about football spectators in the UK

Football is the nation's game, not only for people to watch, but also to take part in. The FA's website says there are:

- *7 million participants, plus 5 million in schools*
- *500,000 volunteers*
- *37,500 clubs, including 9,000 youth clubs*
- *2,000 competitions*
- *32,000 schools who offer football (17,000 primary schools)*
- *30,000 FA-qualified coaches*
- *27,000 FA-qualified referees*
- *45,000 pitches (21,000 facilities).*

● *Local governing bodies of sport* ●

Look again at how football is organised. This will help explain how local governing bodies work. Football in the UK is organised at local level by 43 county football associations who are responsible for organising football in their areas. The various bodies organise their own fixtures and all the players that take part.

GIVE IT A GO: who is your county football association?

Can you find the details of your county football association? Try looking up information on the Internet.

● *Amateur and professional sportspeople* ●

Sport can be played in a number of ways. For some people, sport is an activity that is carried out in their spare time; they are called amateurs. They play sport mainly for enjoyment and receive no money for playing. Some people are good enough to earn money by playing sport, either on a part-time basis, as a semi-professional, or full-time, as a professional. Professional sportsmen and sportswomen can earn huge sums of money either through salaries or prize money. Premiership footballers can earn up to £100,000 per week! However, players in the lower divisions earn much smaller sums, perhaps £600–£700 per week.

Sport's top earners

Sport's top earners	Sport activity	Amount they earnt in 2004
Michael Schumacher	Formula 1	£41.8 million
Tiger Woods	Golf	£37.5 million
Mike Tyson	Boxing	£34 million
Michael Jordan	Basketball	£26.2 million
Grant Hill	Basketball	£18.4 million

GIVE IT A GO: investigating sport associations

1 Choose two sports of your choice – it would be a good idea to choose two of the sports you are going to play.
2 Look up the websites of the associations that govern your chosen sports (you can use a search engine such as Google to do this – a link to this site can be found at www.heinemann.co.uk/hotlinks, express code 0005P).
3 Design and create a poster that shows what these associations do and how your chosen sports are organised. Give examples to illustrate your answer.

• *Regulations* •

Governing bodies also manage the health and safety of players and spectators. Many of the rules that apply to a specific sport are there to make sure players are protected from injury, such as wearing safety equipment. Learn more about sport and leisure rules and regulations in Unit 8, pages 187–189.

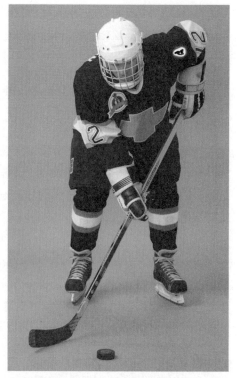

▲ Can you identify the safety equipment this player is wearing?

Resources

In order for you or anybody else to play sport, a range of resources will be needed for the activity to take place.

Some of these resources are in the form of equipment:

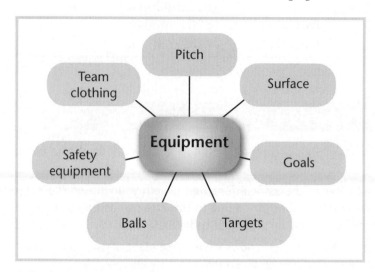

▲ Equipment resources for sport

Some of these resources can be people with specific jobs:

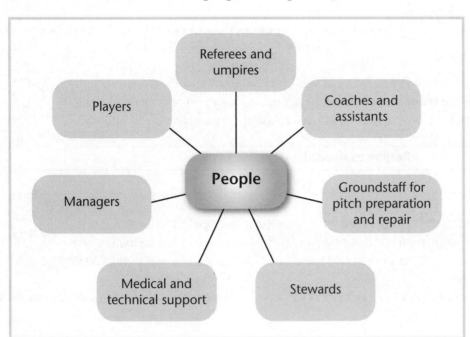

▲ **People resources**

The type of competition or game being played – professional or amateur – will have an effect on the quality of resources needed. For example, two people from your class who decide to play a badminton match are unlikely to need medical staff at the game, although they would need to know where to get medical help if it was needed. However, at a premier-ship football match, enough medical staff and equipment are needed to be able to deal with any emergency situation.

The nature of the sport activity will mean different resources are needed. For example, a swimming gala or athletic competition will need more timekeepers than a basketball or rugby league match. Other resources are needed if there are spectators at the event, such as toilets, refreshments or ticket collectors. Some events will need specialised equipment, such as the Olympic games where world records might be set. Special timing and photographic equipment for close finishes will be needed to accurately record times and distances.

EVIDENCE ACTIVITY

Sport resources

1 Copy out the table below. Make a list of at least ten different sports – make sure that your sport activities are examples of different groups of sport, for example athletic, gymnastic and games. For each sport write down all the resources you would need.

Sport	Resources needed

2 Choose two different sports. Make sure your sports are different, for example, one team sport and one individual sport, or one outdoor and one indoor sport. Draw a table to show all the resources you would need for a game or match and explain why you would need them.

Skills, techniques and components of fitness

When you take part in sport, you will need a lot of different skills to play the sport. You will also need to be fit. The skills and type of fitness you need will depend on the sport you are playing and what your role is in that sport. For example, a goalkeeper in hockey will need different skills and fitness to an outfield player; a gymnast will need different skills and fitness levels compared to a motor racing driver.

Skills

Skills are learned tasks that are needed to take part in sport activities. Some of the skills required in sport include:

- *passing, receiving and controlling a ball or other equipment*
- *throwing, catching, hitting or heading*
- *dribbling with feet or hands*
- *shooting*
- *tumbling and other gymnastic skills*
- *footwork*
- *finding space.*

▲ **What skills is this player using?**

GIVE IT A GO: what skills do you need?

1 Can you think of some examples of skills required in the following sport activities:
- badminton
- swimming
- football
- athletics?

Many skills can be used in a number of different sports. Passing, for example, is needed in football, basketball, netball, rugby and volleyball. Some skills are specific to one sport, such as gymnastic moves – somersaults are needed only in gymnastics.

Sport skills can be **transferable**. For example, learning to pass a basketball will help you become good at passing in netball. This is known as positive transfer. Sometimes learning a skill for one sport can make learning similar skills in another sport harder. This is known as negative transfer. For example, a tennis backhand is similar to a badminton backhand, but if you were a regular tennis player, you might find it difficult to do a badminton backhand properly.

GLOSSARY

Transferable skills are skills that you learn for one sport, but can be used to play a number of others, for example, throwing a cricket ball helps you to learn how to throw a javelin in athletics.

205

CASE STUDY – TRANSFERABLE SKILLS

Nigel Walker, head of the Welsh Sports Council, is an example of an athlete who has been able to transfer sports skills very successfully. As an athlete, he competed in the 110-metre Hurdles event with distinction, gaining 30 international vests for Great Britain. He was also part of the British Olympic team at the Los Angeles Games in 1984. He won bronze medals at both the World and European Indoor Championships in 1987 in the 110m hurdles.

After retiring from athletics, he took up a rugby career, playing as a winger for Cardiff and winning 17 caps for Wales. So how was it that this individual was able to play two different sports to such a high level? Part of the reason was that he was able to *transfer skills* learnt during his athletic career to his new sport of rugby. What skills do you think are common to both sports? Hurdling requires a high degree of co-ordination of the body when travelling over 10 hurdles at speed, as does playing rugby when dodging and weaving between opponents. This would be an example of *positive* transfer of skills. However some skills may have a *negative* effect – in other words, the learning of a skill in athletics makes learning a rugby skill more difficult. For example, in athletics the performer generally needs to repeat a skill a set number of times, such as running over a hurdle ten times. In rugby, the performer must react to the game situation much more and use a wider range of skills.

1   Can you think of any other skills that Nigel Walker will have learnt from athletics that will have helped him to play rugby?

2   Some sports skills have no effect at all. For example, learning to swim breast stroke has no effect on playing snooker. Can you think of some more examples?

3   Can you think of any basic sports skills that a wide range of sports need (for example, catching)?

Techniques

A technique can be described as the way you perform a skill. Some common techniques are:

- dribbling
- hitting
- heading
- throwing and catching
- footwork
- controlling.

Jonny Wilkinson and Charlie Hodgson are both fly halves for the England rugby team. They both need to perform the skill of place kicking, but each player performs the skill in a different way – left or right footed. They can both score drop goals but the way they perform the skill is completely different.

WHAT **if?**

.. players had different techniques?

Try to find examples of players in the same sport performing the same skill differently. Can you describe the differences?

● *Tactics and strategies* ●

Tactics and strategies are the way you play the game or match. For example, a football team might play with a 4–4–2 formation – four defenders, four midfields and two strikers. This strategy may be used if the team you are playing has a particular weakness that you want to use. In tennis, some players like to play on the baseline; this tactic gives the player more time to play shots. It also means that if the player's volleying skill is not very good, they do not need to volley the ball.

The weather might also affect the way you play a game. For example, if there has been a lot of rain and the pitch is muddy, you will need to use different tactics than on a dry pitch.

Tactics and strategies are based on:

- ▭ *your and your team's skill, strengths and weaknesses*
- ▭ *the skill, strengths and weaknesses of your opponent(s)*
- ▭ *the weather conditions*
- ▭ *the kind of sport activity you are playing.*

...it was very windy?

In pairs, make a list of five sport activities that could be affected by the weather. Then write what tactics or strategies could be used for these activities, in bad weather conditions.

Fitness

Fitness has been described, in the Oxford Concise Dictionary, as: 'the ability to undertake everyday activities without undue fatigue'. This means being able to cope with activities without getting too tired.

 THINK ABOUT IT

Choose two members of your family. Describe their current lifestyle. What does a typical day involve? What can you say about their fitness requirements for coping with their everyday activities?

Why would you need more fitness to play sport than to do everyday tasks such as cleaning or walking to the shops? Firstly, the **demands** placed upon your body will be greater. While playing sport you are asking your body to do things it does not normally do. For example, you are lifting greater amounts of weight or moving at faster speeds for longer than normal.

● *What are the components of fitness?* ●

There are a number of different parts that make up fitness. These parts are called the components of fitness.

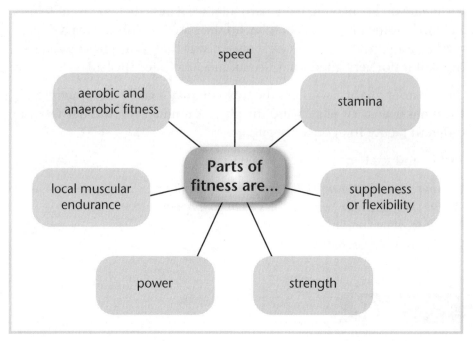

▲ Components of fitness

Speed is your ability to move quickly. A 100-metre sprinter runs the distance in about ten seconds, at an average speed of 22.5 miles per hour. That is fast!

Stamina is the fitness factor that means you can do an activity for a long time. There are different types of stamina, for example, running the Comrades marathon, in South Africa, means you have to be able to keep running for up to 11 hours.

Suppleness, or *flexibility*, is the amount of movement that is possible at a joint – how much it can bend. Gymnasts need to be very supple or flexible to get into some of the positions needed during their routines.

Strength is the name given to your muscles' ability to exert a force to pick things up or move equipment. The athlete in the picture on page 209 needs a lot of strength to be able to pick up weights. The more strength he has, the more weight he can move.

▲ **This man is combining strength and power**

The weightlifter will also need to produce *power*. This fitness factor uses both strength and speed to create power. The faster he lifts the bar above his head, the more power he produces.

Local muscular endurance is a kind of stamina – the ability of particular muscles to do an action for a long time. For example, when performing many sit-ups or press-ups, a small group of muscles is used rather than the whole body.

The final two components of fitness are called **aerobic** and **anaerobic**. Aerobic fitness is how your body turns the oxygen you breathe into energy that helps you take part in sport. For example, long-distance runners use aerobic fitness to help them run at a steady pace – not too fast – and not get out of breath. Anaerobic fitness is how your body uses other energy already stored in your body to help you in sport activities. For example, a 100-metre sprinter uses anaerobic energy; they may even run a 100-metre race without breathing! However, they cannot run much further than 100 metres before they become exhausted and cannot run any more.

All of the above fitness components have one thing in common – they can all be improved with training. They are often called health-related fitness factors.

• *Skill-related components of fitness* •

These are:

- ▭ agility – *the way you move your body into new positions quickly and correctly*
- ▭ co-ordination – *how you move your body and limbs in the correct order to perform a movement or skill*
- ▭ balance – *the way you hold your body in a position without falling over*
- ▭ reaction time – *the time taken to react e.g. to the starter gun in a 100-metre race.*

These components of fitness are ones that cannot always be improved with training; they are abilities you were born with. For example, co-ordination makes sport performers' movements look very easy and smooth, while agility lets you change direction quickly, such as when dodging in and out of cones.

▲ This gymnast is showing both suppleness and balance

• *Relationship between fitness components and sport* •

In all sport activities, the different fitness components you have looked at are linked together. Some sports need lots of strength, while others need more stamina and some need both.

To do well in a sport activity you will need a combination of skills, techniques and fitness. The weight lifter on page 209 needs a lot of strength and power fitness to lift heavy weights. He will need to be mentally tough and able to tell himself that he can lift the weights on the bar, especially if he has never lifted that level of weight before. The weightlifter will also need to have learnt specific skills such as the snatch and the clean and jerk – these are two types of lift. Unlike a long distance runner, the weightlifter does not need to have a lot of stamina or leg speed.

A swimmer needs different skills and fitness that are specific to swimming. There are four different strokes to learn and different ways of starting and turning for different distance events. Swimmers need more stamina and flexibility than weightlifters but less power and strength. Some sport activities are very similar in their requirements, for example basketball and netball need similar catching and passing skills and similar fitness levels.

GIVE IT A GO: what fitness components do you need?

1 In small groups, talk about which fitness components each of the sport activities in the table below need.
2 Copy and complete the table.
3 Compare your results with the other groups. Are they similar?

Sport	Speed	Strength	Stamina	Flexibility	Power	Agility	Reaction Time	Muscular Endurance
Swimming								
Badminton								
Gymnastics								
Netball								
Basketball								
Cricket								

EVIDENCE ACTIVITY

Skills, techniques and fitness

1 Copy and complete the table below for the two sports that you are going to participate in. Fill in the skills, techniques and fitness components you will need for each sport.

	Sport one	Sport two
Skills		
Techniques		
Fitness components		

2 Using the information you gathered for 1, describe why certain skills, techniques and fitness components are important for one of your chosen sports.

Participating in sport

For this unit, you are required to participate in:

- ▭ *one individual sport*
- ▭ *one team sport.*

The sports you choose should contrast each other. This means they should be clearly different – tennis singles and badminton doubles would not be contrasting sports. You may participate in more than two sports but at least two of them must be contrasting. This is a very practical section, it is all about going out and playing your sport activities, learning the rules and regulations, the skills, techniques and types of fitness you need. Have fun!

EVIDENCE ACTIVITY

Participating in sport

1 Participate in two different sports. Write a short report explaining the rules of each of your chosen sports.

2 Using some of the techniques listed on page 213, analyse how well you have played your two chosen sports. Present your results to your class. During your presentation explain the rules of your chosen sports, and tell them some of the tactics you used while participating in your chosen sports.

Reviewing your performance

In order to play sport successfully, you need:

▷ *skills and techniques*
▷ *a knowledge of tactics and strategies*
▷ *fitness.*

If you want to play your sport better you must be able to identify the skills, tactics and fitness components that you are good at, but also be able to identify areas you need to improve on. To help you to improve in your chosen sport, you can set targets of performance. You can check how well you are doing against these targets – this is known as analysing and reviewing your performance.

Analysis of performance

Analyse means to look closely. When taking part in sport, it is important to keep a record of what you have done in each session. This record can say what your strengths and weaknesses are, the skills needed and the fitness levels of the sport. This will help you look closely at your performance and show you what areas you need to work harder at.

When analysing your performance, there are a variety of methods you can use:

▷ *video analysis*
▷ *teacher, coach, peer observation*
▷ *skills tests*
▷ *fitness tests.*

● ***What can you analyse?*** ●

When playing your chosen sports, you can record a number of factors. These might include:

▷ *how many passes you made during a game*
▷ *how many shots, baskets, runs or points you scored in a game*
▷ *how many passes, shots, baskets you missed in a game.*

You can record these facts on a table or graph. Using these results, you can see how well or badly you performed and try to give reasons why. For example, if you start to lose rallies at the end of a badminton match, you could have a low level of stamina The lack of stamina means you are tired before the end of the match, so you cannot put in as much effort to hit the shots. A lack of strength might explain why you strug-gle to beat your opponent on the golf course. Your lack of strength means that you are unable to hit a drive as far and need to take more shots to complete the hole.

Reviewing sport

Reviewing and analysing sport are very similar. Reviewing sport means you are explaining why you have performed in a certain way. When reviewing your performance, you need to understand how particular skills are performed – this is known as a model of performance. For example, in swimming, you can break down the skills into different parts of the swimming action. These are:

- *arm action*
- *leg action*
- *breathing*
- *body position*
- *co-ordination.*

You can then look at each part of the skills and see if you are performing all of them correctly – reviewing your strengths and weaknesses. These models can be found in many sports books or from the sports governing body.

GIVE IT A GO: analysing performance

To understand this better, arrange to watch two people in your class play a sport, such as badminton.

1 Copy the table below onto a sheet of A4 paper and photocopy it.

2 Find a number of people to observe the game.

3 Allow the players to play a game to 21 points. While they are playing the observers should fill out the table.

Practical Sport Assessment Sheet

Player name						
Shot played	Forehand	Backhand	Winning shots	Unforced error	Short serve	Long serve
1						
2						
3						

4 Arrange for one observer to record one of the above types of shot. Once the game has finished, draw a bar chart for each player to compare his or her performance.

5 Now repeat this exercise for a second sport. Design your own assessment sheet and repeat the exercise.

6 What results do you get?

7 What CONCLUSIONS can you draw from these results?

8 How can this help the performer being assessed?

WHAT if?

...I don't have a model of performance?

Visit your two chosen sports' websites. Look for the models of performance. Print or copy them out.

When reviewing your strengths and weaknesses you can use a flow chart to help you. An example for badminton is given below.

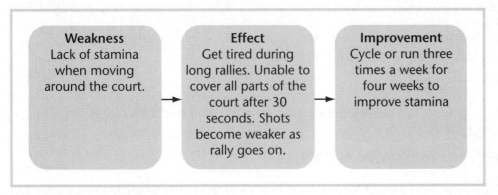

▲ **A review flow chart of badminton**

Setting and monitoring targets

When analysing and reviewing your performance, it is important that you set targets. This way you know what goal you are working towards and it allows you to measure your improvement. For example, you might set a target of improving your best time for the 800-metres running race by 5 percent. If your best time is 1 minute 55 seconds, then you could set a target of 1 minute 49 seconds. With this target in mind, you will train to try to run faster. When training you can time yourself to see if you are getting faster or not. When setting targets, remember to make them SMART targets (read Unit 3, pages 75–76 to recap setting SMART targets).

• *Effects of strengths and weaknesses on performance* •

The strengths and weaknesses that exist in your performance in your chosen sport can have a variety of effects. A lack of fitness could affect your ability to complete the whole match or game without getting too tired. A lack of skill will mean that you may be forced to play in a particular way or only at a particular level, for example, having a weak backhand in tennis might mean that you will struggle to win matches because you can only play well on one side of the court.

When you set your training targets you need to think of how your weaknesses affect your performance. You can then work on improving your weaknesses so that you can reach your training targets.

EVIDENCE ACTIVITY

Reviewing and analysing your performance

For each of your two chosen sports, keep a sport diary. You can include the results of skills or fitness tests, video or photo analysis, personal or peer observations or even certificates and medals. Try to keep this diary for two months.

1 After each match or training session, write a short review of your performance during that session. Write what you think your strengths and weaknesses are.

2 In your sport diary:

   a describe how your strengths and weaknesses have affected your performance at any match or training session

   b write a list of the things you could do to change.

3 Write a report in your sport diary that explains how your strengths and weaknesses have affected your performance. In this report discuss how you can improve your skills, techniques and fitness.

Find the answers to the questions in the puzzle. They could be written across, down or diagonally, backwards or forwards.

```
T A Q T W S K R D R E E Z W T A C T I C S T S
B E P R Q Y U E I O A P A S D Y E H K F S V A
G C A H U I E J T E C H N I Q U E S C E X N F
D P R M K P L S M B O D S P N T R B H V E A E
E S C H S C Z S Q N A E W S X Y P S P R H N T
E P G O V P R O F E S S I O N A L S N O U S Y
P E I L R M O N H Y K M T G B T V K C B W S K
S F V T R O E R D A Q U G O V I C X T X S W Q
K W C R C T B Y T U E E E U I O C L O S E D O
G T H T P H I L O S K J N H G N F D N V D A T
C A I S P Z J N T R X C R O B V G B A S N P R
T E M O T E P A K O F I F A I I O E U S P U C
P R Y T N R E E E P B N C E S K V E E W R Q H
Q O F F I C I A L S O P T O C H L Q U S M U K
C B S S O I J N B S D F I T N E S S T E S T S
H I Q H S U P R Y Q U S G V E V C F C T A T R
D C U S M A R T Q A Z P R W O S N X K E D C G
P O S I T I V E S K I L L S T R A N S F E R C
V F R G Y E E J R I Q F T O N P F G P I D P N
N A T I O N A L G O V E R N I N G B O D I E S
```

1 Basketball and hockey are both _____.

2 Players who are paid to play are called _____.

3 The _____ are responsible for each sport within the country.

4 _____ is important in sport, which is why players wear shin pads and gum shields.

5 Referees, linesmen and judges are all _____.

6 In order to play a sport well, you need to learn many _____.

7 The abbreviation for the international governing body for football is _____.

8 When a skill learnt in one sport helps you learn a similar skill in another sport, we say there has been a _____.

9 The opposite of an open skill is a _____ skill.

10 In order to defeat your opponent, you need to use _____.

11 Your ability to move quickly is called your _____.

12 Exercise that uses oxygen to produce energy is called _____.

13 You can use _____ to analyse your performance.

14 If you set targets they should be _____.

15 Football and rugby are both played on a _____.

unit 10

Introducing customer service

In this unit you will look at the basic ideas about customer service and why it is important in the sport and leisure industry. You will learn about customers and their needs, the importance of presentation in delivering good customer service and of having good communication skills. You will also have the chance to practise and develop your customer care skills in a variety of situations.

This unit is internally assessed. This means, to pass this unit, you will complete an assignment set and marked by your tutor. Many of the assessment criteria can be covered through practical activities, such as a period of work placement or role-play exercises, rather than by using written assessments.

In this unit you will need to learn about:

▭ different types of customers and their needs and expectations
▭ preparing yourself and your work area for customer service
▭ good communication skills
▭ providing good care and service to your customers.

Different types of customers

Sport and leisure are known as service industries. This means that they give customers things to do, such as going for a swim, watching a film at the cinema or eating out at a restaurant. If organisations are to be successful, it is very important that customers visit more than once. Service industries rely on **repeat business**. This means customers use the services more than once and they tell their friends and family about how good it was, so that more customers use the service.

WHAT if?

...customers only visited Alton Towers once?

Discuss what would happen if people only went to Alton Towers once and never went again. What would this mean for the organisation?

● *What is a customer?* ●

A customer is anybody who uses an organisation's goods and services. Sport and leisure organisations try to attract many different types of customers. They want as many customers as possible and to keep them as customers for as long as possible. For example, a health club wants lots of members and wants them to be members for a long time.

GIVE IT A GO: different types of customers

In the following word search, there are 15 types of customers. Can you find them?

```
A  D  U  L  T  U  I  N  T  E  R  N  A  L  C
C  O  L  L  E  G  E  S  W  C  J  W  Z  B  F
B  S  I  N  G  L  E  P  A  R  E  N  T  L  A
F  M  U  Y  A  R  A  H  E  H  D  F  C  T  M
T  E  E  N  A  G  E  R  O  T  I  A  F  X  I
C  Z  L  S  N  C  R  W  C  R  S  Z  R  T  L
E  O  D  M  E  M  B  E  R  S  A  E  Y  G  I
A  A  E  B  P  Q  Z  S  S  H  B  F  C  R  E
F  O  R  E  I  G  N  E  R  S  L  B  I  O  S
P  Q  L  J  C  H  I  L  D  R  E  N  I  U  B
N  M  Y  C  X  A  E  G  V  C  D  S  E  P  W
K  Z  R  E  B  U  S  I  N  E  S  S  E  S  C
S  C  H  O  O  L  S  E  X  T  E  R  N  A  L
```

Did you find them?

1 adult	**6** teenager	**11** schools
2 internal	**7** foreigners	**12** colleges
3 external	**8** elderly	**13** groups
4 families	**9** children	**14** disabled
5 single parent	**10** businesses	**15** members.

Internal customers

Internal customers are people who work for an organisation. They are also customers because they are using the facilities or buying their own company's goods, for example you may be a ticket collector at a cinema, but you may also watch films there in your spare time. Internal customers should be treated in exactly the same way as any other customer of the organisation. Internal customers are as important as other customers as they are the people you work with. How you are treated by others can affect the way you respond to and work with people in the future.

External customers

External customers are all the other people who use the goods, services and facilities of an organisation. For example, an external customer can be someone who is paying to use the facilities of a gym or health club, who needs help or advice from a fitness instructor, information on a meal from a waitress or directions from a receptionist in a hotel.

External customers also include visitors to a centre and other workers carrying out repairs or maintenance to the facility.

Some customers may have specific needs that need to be met – they may have a sensory disability (hearing or sight impairment) or be physically disabled. In all cases, it is important that staff meet customer needs quickly, efficiently and in a way that does not cause offence.

Needs

People will become customers because they have a **need**. We all have basic needs, like food, shelter, clothes and drink. As a student you might need to get a qualification because you would like a particular job or career. We also have other needs such as information, enquiries or the need to buy certain goods or services. The sport and leisure industry answers people's needs.

GIVE IT A GO: why do people become customers?

1 Think about the last time you went to a shop or leisure centre as a customer.
2 Write down the reasons you went to that particular place, for example, why did you go to a sport centre, a library or an amusement park?

GIVE IT A GO: playing badminton

Imagine you have gone to a sport centre to play badminton. Make a list of five reasons why you would play badminton at a sport centre.

There are many reasons why you would play badminton at a sport centre rather than setting up a net at home. For example:

- *you might go to learn how to play the game from an instructor*
- *the centre may offer a crèche where you can leave your young child*
- *the centre may have a team that plays in local leagues and competitions*
- *the centre might be the cheapest one for badminton in the area*
- *the centre might have the best facilities*
- *the centre might be near to where you live*
- *you might want to keep fit*
- *you might want to meet new people or socialise with friends.*

▲ **You might want to play badminton at a leisure centre so you can meet new friends**

GIVE IT A GO: needs

A leisure centre tries to meet these customer needs in a number of different ways.

1 Take each of the reasons for playing badminton you wrote down for the *Give it a go* activity on page 222.

2 Think how a leisure centre might try to meet that need. For example, the centre might offer coaching classes by employing a coach for people who want to learn to play.

● *Meeting customer needs* ●

Sport and leisure organisations want to have as many different customers as possible, each with different sport and leisure needs. In order to keep their customers the organisation must try to meet all their customers' needs.

How can an organisation meet the needs of lots of different people? Think about a multi-screen cinema – there are a large number of screens all showing different films, at different times. This way the cinema can meet the needs of customers with different tastes in films and who want to watch at different times. A sports centre will have a wide range of sport activities during the week to make sure that all their customers have something they enjoy doing – activities for children during the afternoon, ladies-only swimming and swimming lessons for beginners. By offering the right activity at the right time and at the right price, organisations hope to attract a wide range of customers.

CASE STUDY – A FAMILY DAY OUT

The Harris family have decided to go out for the day to a theme park. The family consists of Mr and Mrs Harris, who are both in their 40s, Stephanie Harris who is 19 and Matthew who is 17. In order that they all enjoy themselves, they want to choose a park where they will all have something to do.

1 For each member of the family, list some of the needs you think they might have while at the theme park.

2 How might the theme park cater for these different needs?

3 If Matthew and Stephanie were 7 and 9 respectively, how might the family's needs change?

GLOSSARY

Expectations are beliefs about what will happen or what something is.

Customer expectations

Customers have **expectations**. You will have had expectations about this course, a holiday resort you have been to or a product you have bought. Customers expect a number of basic things, such as:

- *receiving good customer care from the organisation*
- *both the organisation and staff creating the right impression*
- *getting prompt attention from the organisation*
- *getting appropriate and easy-to-understand communications from both the organisation and its staff.*

For example, customers at a restaurant will expect:

- *the restaurant to be clean and tidy*
- *the food to be safe to eat*
- *staff to be helpful and well presented*
- *the prices to be reasonable.*

▲ Restaurant customers expect the food to be safe to eat

WHAT if?

...my expectations were not met?

In small groups, tell each other about occasions when your expectations about a product or service were not met. Did you recommend the product or service to your friends and family? Will you use the same product or service again?

GIVE IT A GO: failing to meet customer expectations

1 Copy and complete the following table giving the reasons for and consequences of not meeting customer expectations. An example has been done for you.

Customer expectations	Reasons for not meeting these expectations	Consequences
Customer expects good customer service	Lack of staff training or experience	Customer receives a poor experience and does not return. Organisation loses business
Customers expect the right impression to be made to them		
Customers expect to be dealt with promptly		
Customers receive clear and appropriate communication		

2 Can you think of more examples? Discuss these in small groups.

By giving good customer service and meeting or, even better, exceeding customer expectations, organisations will benefit from:

▭ *a good reputation*
▭ *repeat business from their customers*
▭ *new customers*
▭ *increased profits and a more successful organisation*
▭ *motivated and happier staff*
▭ *less complaints from customers.*

CASE STUDY – EVERYONE IS A CUSTOMER

Mr Shilling is a teacher at a large comprehensive school where he teaches sport studies. As he works, he comes into contact with lots of different people – other teachers he works with including Anita, Sally and Frank, caretakers and senior members of staff like the head teacher and of course his pupils.

1 When and how is he an internal customer and what needs might he have?

2 When does Mr Shilling provide customer service to others?

3 What expectations might Mr Shilling have when he is a customer and what expectations might colleagues have of Mr Shilling?

EVIDENCE ACTIVITY

1 Choose a sport or leisure services provider.

2 Think about what needs and expectations different customers of this organisation will have.

3 Write a short report which describes the organisation, identifies different types of customer and discusses the needs and expectations of these customers.

Preparing yourself and your work area

GLOSSARY

Impressions are feelings or opinions you have about a person or organisation. They are based on things like how they respond to you, how they look or how they talk to you.

First **impressions** are very important if you want to give customers the idea that you and your organisation are professional and helpful. If you prepare yourself then you will always be able to help a customer quickly and give them the correct information.

Preparing yourself

● *Personal appearance* ●

One of the first impressions a customer will have of you and your organisation is based on your personal appearance, including your personal presentation. The way you look and the way you interact with customers will make a lasting impression and affect the expectations a customer has of an organisation. Even before you have spoken to customers, they form an impression of you and the facility. For example, if you are dressed neatly and professionally and smile at a customer as they come in, they will feel at ease and will expect good service. It has been said that this happens within as little as 10 seconds! So it is very important that the impression you make is positive!

▲ **First impressions are often lasting impressions**

○○ THINK ABOUT IT

Look at the picture of a hotel receptionist. What points can you see that would help to make a positive impression? Is the receptionist:

- clean and tidy
- smartly dressed
- smiling?

Is her:

- desk tidy and well organised, making things easy to find
- work area professional and friendly looking?

All of these factors help create a positive image of both the organisation and the receptionist.

Your personal presentation will also play an important part in providing a positive image to customers.

...the chef at a restaurant has dirty fingernails?

In small groups, list some factors about a chef that would put you off your meal.

Did you include:

- dirty chef's whites (his uniform)
- dirty fingernails
- unshaven
- dirty hair
- poor personal hygiene (perhaps he smells!)?

Dress codes

For certain jobs, there is a standard dress code or uniform. For example, chefs often wear chef's whites, including a tall hat to make sure that hair does not get into the food. Lifeguards may wear red and yellow shorts and a T-shirt to make them easily visible in a crowded swimming pool. Uniforms have a number of different roles:

- *provide protection for the employee*
- *make it easy to recognise staff of an organisation*
- *create a professional and recognisable image for the organisation.*

Posture

When dealing with customers, be aware of your posture. Posture is how you hold your body, for example the way you stand at a counter or sit at your desk. Slouching in front of customers gives an impression that you do not care about them or meeting their needs. Having the right posture is an important part of creating the right impression. It also helps you to keep your body healthy and feel confident.

▲ **Which person would you prefer to be served by?**

● *Personal qualities* ●

Your personal presentation and appearance are only two parts of delivering good customer service. Having a positive attitude to your work and towards customers is also very important in a service industry like sport and leisure. You need to show you are happy to help people. You must care for your customers and have a positive attitude to their needs and expectations.

Another personal quality that will help you to deliver good customer service is that of teamwork. This involves working well together to complete tasks.

● *Knowledge* ●

Many customers need information or guidance when they talk to you. They may ask questions like: 'What time does the swimming pool close?', 'How much does this cost?' or 'Are these shoes suitable for playing badminton?' It is essential, as an employee, to know the answers to any questions a customer might have. If you don't know the answers, you need to know where to find them or which other members of staff will know. Teamwork is important here as another team member may know the answer to a customer's question. Do not give wrong information. Where possible, keep any lists of information close at hand so that you can refer to them when asked about products or services.

● *Knowledge of products and services* ●

Knowledge of products and services is an important feature of customer service. It is important for staff to be able to respond quickly and accurately to customer requests for information, advice and guidance, without being referred to someone else. For example, a receptionist at a hotel should be able to describe the different rooms available and the tariffs that apply. A lifeguard should know the times the swimming pool opens and closes. A waitress in a restaurant should know about the content of the meals on offer. This would be of particular importance to someone with an allergy!

● *Guidelines* ●

Organisations will issue guidelines to staff on a variety of issues, such as customer care. For example, a guideline could be that the telephone must be answered within five rings or that a complaint must be responded to within 48 hours. By having guidelines, staff will know what is expected of them in a particular situation. For organisations that operate a number of outlets, for instance McDonalds restaurants, it helps to ensure that customers receive the same standard of service in every outlet.

● *Standards of service* ●

Customer service also requires standards of service to be written down. If an organisation has standards, it will be able to measure how well customer service is being delivered and how well the organisation is performing. It also allows customers to know exactly what they can expect from an organisation.

● *Teamwork* ●

Underpinning all customer service activities is teamwork. Staff in the sport and leisure sector need to work together so that the customer can receive the best possible service.

◯ THINK ABOUT IT

Think about your school or college. What are the benefits of the reception staff, canteen staff, teaching staff and library staff all working towards the same goal? Who will ultimately benefit?

Preparing your work area

In the same way that your personal appearance can say a lot about you and your organisation, so will your own work space. It should be neat and tidy with everything in its place, so that it can be found quickly when needed. All space should be used appropriately and not wasted, such as putting all pencils in a proper holder.

A disorganised work area might mean:

- ▢ *items become lost or damaged*
- ▢ *injuries occur because the area is unsafe*
- ▢ *a customer seeing the area assumes the person who works there is disorganised*
- ▢ *fires or a spillage can happen easily. For example, in the chemical store of a swimming pool, if chemicals are stored incorrectly.*

● *Health and safety* ●

Health and safety regulations will have an effect on how certain areas of work are organised and the equipment within that area. (Read more about health and safety regulations on pages 119–124.)

GIVE IT A GO: safe working areas

1 In small groups, visit a part of your school or college – a classroom or the sports hall.

2 Make a list of any hazards you see in the area. For example, are there any trip hazards?

3 Report your findings back to the rest of the class.

Duty of care

The Health and Safety at Work Act (1971) was introduced to reduce the number of accidents in the workplace. As an employee, you have a duty of care to others (read Unit 2, pages 36–37). This means you have to make sure that you are behaving in a way that does not put your team members and customers at risk. This includes not touching safety equipment, wearing the correct clothing while at work and reporting any problems you discover. When you start work, you will receive health and safety training to help promote good standards of health and safety.

EVIDENCE ACTIVITY

1 Write two or three paragraphs to explain how you would prepare yourself to face customers. P2

2 Write two or three paragraphs to explain how you would prepare your work area for customer service. P3

Communication skills

Communication is about giving and receiving information. It is important to give information in a way that makes sure that the other person understands the information correctly.

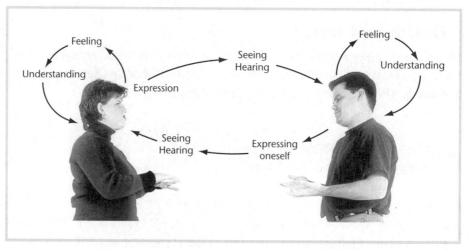

▲ **The communication cycle**

Types of communication

There are various types communication.

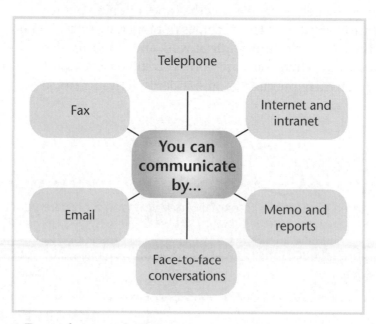

▲ **Types of communication**

Verbal and non-verbal communication skills

There are two main ways of communicating: verbal and non-verbal. Verbal communication is anything that you say or write down. Non-verbal communication is the way you communicate and the messages you send out without saying or writing anything. Verbal and non-verbal communication work together to give people information. For example, when you are talking to someone face-to-face you give them information through your words, your hand gestures, your tone of voice and your body language.

● *Non-verbal communication skills* ●

Non-verbal communication skills include facial expressions, body language, tone of voice and the wide variety of gestures you make all the time. When you are talking to someone face-to-face, your expressions and gestures send out a meaning.

▲ **Some commonly used gestures in the UK**

THINK ABOUT IT

Is this person showing:

a genuine warmth to someone or

b is he irritated with them?

How would you feel if a member of staff looked at you like this when dealing with a request?

Much of your time dealing with customers in the workplace will be face-to-face. You have already learnt that your personal presentation is very important. Your body language will also communicate with the customer. The way you stand, your **posture** and the expression on your face will all send out a message to the customer. It is important that you think about the overall impression you are creating when dealing with customers.

Your body language, the things you say without speaking, is very important in creating that first impression. It is important to make eye contact with a customer – it shows you are interested in them and what they have to say.

GIVE IT A GO: making eye contact

1 In pairs, decide who is to be the interviewer and who is going to be interviewed. You have five minutes to discuss any topic of your choice. You must maintain eye contact for as long as possible.

2 What did you find difficult? Why did you find it difficult?

When using the telephone, it is important to have the same expression and gesture as you would if you were communicating face-to-face. By smiling when using the phone, you will send a positive image through your voice.

• *Verbal communication skills* •

Using the correct format when communicating verbally or in writing is very important, as it sends out a professional impression.

When communicating verbally, always start with welcoming, polite introductions, for example: 'Good morning, my name is Ishmael, how can I help you?' If you are face-to-face with the customer, remember that you are also communicating non-verbally – make sure you look at the customer and smile! Do not be too familiar with the customer. Do not refer to them by their first name unless you know them personally. You can call a customer Sir or Madam if you do not have their names. Try to make sure that the impression you give is warm and welcoming.

When using written communication, such as letters, memos and emails, it is important that what you write is clear and easy to understand. Spelling and grammar are an important part of getting the message right. If your spelling and grammar are poor, ask a team member to read through your communication before you send it out.

EVIDENCE ACTIVITY

1 With a partner, talk about what things are important when you communicate with customers and why.

2 Make a list of the most important points.

Care and service to customers

As you have seen, customer service is a very important part of the sport and leisure industry. The success of an organisation depends on customers using products and services again and again. It is often said that a happy customer might tell one other person about a positive experience they have had, but an unhappy customer will tell ten people about their bad experience! It is much easier to keep existing customers than it is to attract new ones.

Care

Customer service is also about caring for customers. Your attitude plays an important role in how you look after and care for your customers. If you do not care then this will be reflected in the customer service and help you give them.

Showing a customer you care for them involves all of the points you have learnt about already in this unit. When dealing with customers, you must make sure that you meet customers' needs and expectations. When you are dealing with customers, make eye contact, have a positive posture and allow the customer to speak while you listen. To show you have understood them, repeat the customers' problem or question back to them.

If the customer needs information or advice, make sure that you give them the correct information **promptly** and **courteously**. If you tell a customer that you will do something make sure you do it – if you promise a customer a written response to a complaint in five days, then you must send your response within five days not six!

Service

When providing customer service to people, it is important that the level of service is always the same. Customers do not want to know that you are not feeling well or that there is a problem with a piece of equipment in the building. How can you make sure that the service is the same? Often, organisations will have a written set of standards, or a charter, which sets out the level of customer service that is promised. An example is shown on page 237 for the Sports Department of Birmingham City – a link is available at www.heinemann.co.uk/hotlinks (express code 0005P).

GLOSSARY

Promptly means doing something without delay.
Courteously means being polite and considerate when dealing with people.

Our Mission Statement

To create a dynamic sport and leisure service that makes a difference to people's lives by offering high quality, healthy lifestyles and sporting opportunities, which are accessible, affordable and the envy of others.

These are the service standards that you can expect

1. Choice
We will offer an extensive choice of activities for a broad range of abilities, either directly or in working with other organisations.

2. Equality
We will actively encourage participation from all sections of the community and seek ways of improving access and provision for everyone. We will respect people's individuality and ask that customers have respect for one another.

3. Facilities, open on time and ready to receive you
Facilities will be opened and activities will commence at published times. We will be ready to receive you, with all equipment and related services in working order.

4. Clean and tidy facilities
All facilities, including outdoor areas and car parks, will be clean and tidy. To help us achieve this please notify a member of staff of any area with which you are not happy.

5. A safe and comfortable environment
We will take all reasonable and practical steps to protect your health, safety and security, including adherence to all relevant Health and Safety legislation and guidelines. Facilities will be maintained at the appropriate levels.

6. Courteous, helpful and trained staff
Staff will provide a warm and friendly welcome, be well presented and wear name badges. All staff will be appropriately trained and hold relevant qualifications.

7. Value for Money
We will aim to provide activities and programmes at affordable prices that offer value for money. This will include different payment options or methods. Reduced prices for a wide range of target groups will be available through the Passport to Leisure scheme.

8. Information and openness
Information on opening times, activities and prices will be available in all reception areas, through the Corporate Contact Centre and via the website. You will be kept informed about our performance against the Customer Charter standards.

9. Customer consultation
We will actively consult with users and non-users regarding the service we provide and your views will be positively welcomed.

10. Effective handling of complaints
We will respond to any service complaints within 5 working days. If you are unhappy with any aspect of the service, please speak to a member of staff who will try to resolve your concerns immediately or complete a Customer Comments form.

If you experience any problems with the service provided, or have any comments to make, please speak to the duty manager. Alternatively, please write down your suggestion, complaint, compliment or comment on a Customer Comments form available in the reception area.

▲ **A Mission Statement outlines the level of service customers can expect**

By putting their customer service standards in writing, the Birmingham City Council can check that they are achieving these standards. It also means that customers know what to expect every time they visit a council facility.

GIVE IT A GO: student charters

1 Find out if your school or college has a student charter.

2 In pairs, read the student charter and discuss why it is important.

● *Assisting customers* ●

In the sport and leisure sector, service involves providing customers with assistance; helping them. You may do this in a number of ways, such as by giving directions to a room or activity, helping a person with their luggage, ordering a taxi or arranging to safeguard a person's valuables in a hotel. There are many situations where you may be required to assist a customer using the products and services of your organisation.

⬭ THINK ABOUT IT

Can you think of occasions when you have needed assistance? How did the staff help you? Did they do enough? What else could they have done?

Sometimes you may need to advise a customer to visit other providers. For example, a general sports clothing shop may not stock training shoes that are specifically suited to running a marathon, in which case you could direct the customer to a specialist outlet that has what he or she needs.

● *Providing products and services* ●

Customer service involves making available the products or services that the organisation sells or provides. For example, if you work in a sports clothing outlet, you will need to have available different types and sizes of shoes suitable for different activities. You need to know about the products and services on offer and be able to provide customers with a choice, as well as with explanations about the differences between different products and brands, for example.

● *Responding to changing customer needs* ●

As a member of staff at a health club, you might help a customer to tone up by providing and monitoring an exercise programme. As this customer progresses and becomes fitter, you will need to respond to his or her changing needs by modifying the programme they are following, so they can continue to progress and improve. You might also need to be aware of changes in fashion and trends, changes in a customer's lifestyle or new products and services that may be of interest to the customer.

• *Seeking assistance when required* •

In some situations, it may be necessary for you to ask for help from another member of staff who has more knowledge and experience than yourself in order to ensure that a customer receives the best advice and guidance. This may be from a colleague or your supervisor.

• *Organisational limitations* •

In customer service, it is important that you operate within the limits of the organisation. Advice must be free from bias and must conform to all relevant regulations and codes of practice. For example, you cannot offer products or services that the organisation does not actually provide. You cannot offer services outside the normal opening hours of the organisation. You cannot go against any safety regulations or guidelines. For example, there may be an age limit (such as 18 for sun beds) or height limit (such as in an amusement park) that you must keep to for certain equipment.

• *Keeping records and information* •

It is important for an organisation to keep records and information about any dealings with customers. This helps with monitoring customers in order to keep them happy and to attract new customers. For example, is a customer making the correct progress towards a stated goal? Is a customer exceeding the recommended use of a particular product? Are customers aware of new products and services that might be relevant to them? The operation of a facility should also be supported by written records, such as recording the water conditions in a swimming pool. These procedures all help an organisation to deliver high standards of customer care.

The following are some important things to remember for good customer service.

Do:

- *offer help when you think it is needed*
- *maintain eye contact at all times*
- *speak clearly and with a polite tone of voice*
- *listen to customers*
- *smile at all times when dealing with customers*
- *show initiative – do not wait to be asked.*

Don't:

- *over-promise and under-deliver*
- *give out incorrect or inaccurate information to customers*
- *dismiss customer complaints – the customer is always right!*

EVIDENCE ACTIVITY

1 Choose **two** sport or leisure organisations where there is a customer service area, for example, the reception area in a sports club or the information desk at a theme park. (If you have a job or work experience in the sport and leisure sector, then you can do this activity in a real situation, rather than using role play.)

2 Write a list of the kinds of customers you will have to deal with and any problems or questions they are likely to have.

3 Make a list of what you will need in order to get yourself and your workplace ready for serving customers. (Don't forget about health and safety!)

4 Work with a partner, or with your teacher, to role play dealing with a customer in your chosen organisation.

5 Write about your role play.

   a Write a paragraph about how you gave good and consistent customer service.

   b Write another paragraph explaining why good customer service is important.

Find the answers to the questions in the puzzle. They could be written across, down or diagonally, backwards or forwards.

C	W	L	J	M	X	A	I	O	S	M	I	L	E	Q	J	D	D	B	G	C	E	C	C
P	U	V	R	V	B	E	A	M	I	T	Y	V	B	N	A	B	W	A	R	M	Z	O	J
S	W	S	I	J	P	P	R	O	M	P	T	L	Y	D	M	T	R	T	E	D	A	M	O
P	M	D	T	B	W	R	K	X	C	E	M	H	A	L	T	Q	F	Z	E	H	R	P	X
R	A	S	V	O	A	A	E	Y	E	C	O	N	T	A	C	T	L	E	T	H	N	L	C
O	V	E	R	Y	M	T	B	E	U	L	D	A	Q	Z	I	B	U	A	I	T	C	A	M
M	I	J	D	R	B	E	X	P	E	C	T	A	T	I	O	N	S	U	N	Y	D	I	D
I	K	H	O	S	H	J	R	U	O	L	F	V	I	B	P	S	W	C	G	R	R	N	E
S	R	E	G	Y	I	B	D	S	N	I	A	D	H	H	S	H	T	S	K	E	U	P	J
E	L	A	N	D	S	A	F	E	T	Y	Q	B	L	M	Z	C	S	U	H	C	S	W	Z
Z	I	L	D	H	B	A	B	L	S	X	G	O	A	E	Q	I	O	D	S	L	P	H	C
V	N	T	W	I	C	F	M	A	Q	P	I	D	N	D	R	T	I	U	A	F	Y	B	H
K	O	H	I	S	B	G	A	N	D	Y	T	Y	G	X	C	E	N	H	R	R	J	W	A
Y	Q	B	M	I	E	H	U	Q	D	C	S	U	U	I	E	A	E	J	D	T	C	Y	N
L	A	K	Z	C	P	O	Y	T	L	I	I	V	A	L	A	T	E	H	A	R	E	J	G
O	I	M	P	R	E	S	S	I	O	N	L	U	G	N	G	C	D	R	I	B	Y	S	O
E	T	V	L	Y	K	P	M	P	F	A	S	W	E	I	D	R	S	M	H	N	E	C	Y
D	M	C	B	O	E	K	K	E	X	P	R	O	G	U	S	J	B	E	X	L	F	A	H
E	I	R	A	R	U	N	D	W	J	O	T	B	Y	E	Z	L	N	P	K	B	I	S	J
U	N	D	E	R	S	T	O	O	D	I	A	Q	D	A	T	T	I	T	U	D	E	F	R

1   People who use products and services are called _____.

2   All customers have _____ that we try to meet.

3   It is important that these are met by an organisation

4   An organisation hopes to give the right _____ to customers?

5   If customers are happy they will not _____.

6   When dealing with a customer always try to _____.

7   A way of communicating without talking.

8   Legislation that keeps everyone safe at work.

9   Effective communication means that the communication is _____.

10   When dealing with a customer start with a _____.

11   Customers will expect to be treated with _____.

12   Complaints should be dealt with _____.

13   Good customer service is all about having the right _____.

14   Always maintain this when dealing with customers.

15   Never what to a customer?

Word search answers

Unit 1

1 leisure **2** health club **3** commercial **4** volunteers **5** partnership
6 franchise **7** services **8** shift system **9** seasonal **10** operational **11** role
12 teamwork **13** social commitments **14** qualifications **15** manager

Unit 2

1 contract **2** working time regulations **3** perks **4** induction **5** negligence
6 hazards **7** data protection **8** appraisal **9** grievance **10** redundancy

Unit 3

1 health **2** fitness **3** skeletal **4** tendons **5** oxygen **6** carbohydrates
7 calcium **8** nutrients **9** SMART **10** balanced

Unit 4

1 Connections **2** vocational **3** interpersonal **4** transferable **5** SMART
6 covering **7** advertisement **8** personal **9** portfolio **10** interview

Unit 5

1 recycling **2** global warming **3** biodegradable **4** filter systems
5 food hygiene **6** walking **7** ethically **8** HASAWA **9** discrimination
10 RIDDOR

Unit 6

1 employee **2** self-employed **3** overtime **4** pay advice **5** gross
6 National Insurance **7** benefits **8** means testing **9** interest
10 Child Benefit **11** budget **12** bank account **13** black **14** expenditure
15 bills

Unit 7

Page 153
1 fashion show **2** cup **3** league **4** world cup **5** round robin **6** raffle
7 quiz **8** car boot sale **9** fête **10** ladder **11** concert **12** exhibition

Page 170
1 communicate **2** resources **3** working with others **4** plan **5** budget
6 duty of care **7** venue **8** customer service **9** agenda **10** evaluated
11 chairperson **12** contingency **13** staff **14** licence **15** car boot sale

Unit 8

1 segmentation **2** Paralympics **3** EIS **4** bridge **5** FA **6** Sport England
7 equitable **8** fairness **9** obese **10** hallmark

Unit 9

1 team sports **2** professionals **3** national governing bodies **4** safety
5 officials **6** techniques **7** FIFA **8** positive skills transfer **9** closed **10** tactics
11 speed **12** aerobic **13** fitness tests **14** SMART **15** pitch

Unit 10

1 customers **2** needs **3** expectations **4** impression **5** complain **6** smile
7 body language **8** health and safety **9** understood **10** warm greeting
11 courtesy **12** promptly **13** attitude **14** eye contact **15** over-promise

Index